# Praise for *INTEGRITY*
# by Dr. Henry Cloud

• • • • • • • • • • • • • • • • • • • •

"The best of the bunch... [*Integrity*] is engaging, and the principles and writing are clear... [*Integrity*] lays out a transparent way to be a terrific leader by drawing on and improving your best traits."

—*The New York Times*

"An insightful examination of the elements of character that contribute to success in life and business... With *Integrity*, Cloud... has straddled the worlds of interpersonal relationships and business leadership and provided valuable guidance for success."

—*The Boston Globe*

"Living in a world with assigned roles, rather than with an authentic self, drains you of the critical life energy you need for the constructive pursuit of things that you truly value. Dr. Cloud's new book will show you how to get past your assigned roles and into the integrity of an authentic self which can produce the results you are looking for in your work and in your personal life."

—Dr. Phil McGraw, #1 *New York Times* best-selling author and host of the *Dr. Phil* show

"The number-one characteristic that people want leaders to demonstrate is integrity—people who walk their talk and lead a life of character. In *Integrity*, Henry Cloud looks at those 'personal issues' that make people successful by giving them a path to follow. Let Henry Cloud teach you how to live an authentic life. This is a must-read!"

"Dr. Henry Cloud is an expert in helping leaders see how their character development is essential to their effectiveness."

"If business leaders had the insight and character Dr. Cloud describes here, we would have better run and more effective companies."

"Integrity may be the least understood attribute among business leaders. Dr. Cloud shows that success in business is about trust, having the courage to face our own weaknesses and to better understand those around us. A valuable approach that should be practiced by anyone in a leadership position, Dr. Cloud makes it clear that strength of character, or integrity, is the only source of sustainable results."

# integrity

## the courage to meet
## the demands of reality

# Dr. Henry Cloud

HARPER

NEW YORK • LONDON • TORONTO • SYDNEY

I dedicate this book, with gratitude,
to the leaders who have allowed me into their lives,
companies, and dilemmas. As you have hammered
out the difficult demands of reality,
I have learned from you.


And to my father, who showed me that
business and integrity go hand in hand.

HARPER

INTEGRITY. © 2006 by Dr. Henry Cloud. All rights reserved. Printed in the United States of America. No part of this book may be used or reproduced in any manner whatsoever without written permission except in the case of brief quotations embodied in critical articles and reviews. For information, address HarperCollins Publishers, 195 Broadway, New York, NY 10007.

HarperCollins books may be purchased for educational, business, or sales promotional use. For information, please e-mail the Special Markets Department at SPsales@harpercollins.com.

First Harper Paperback edition published 2009

Library of Congress Cataloging-in-Publication Data is available upon request.

ISBN 978-0-06-084969-6

23 24 25 26 27  LBC  36 35 34 33 32

# contents

# CONTENTS

# acknowledgments

Thanks to all of my consulting clients over the years. You know who you are, and you have taught me much. I have been fortunate to witness your character and have it affect my own.

Thanks to Jan Miller, my literary agent, and her other arm, Shannon Miser-Marven. From the initial breakfast, you had passion for this project, and have continued to see it through. Your professionalism is unequaled, and you have brought it all to fruition. Besides that, you guys are fun.

Thanks to Marion Maneker at HarperCollins. You "got it" from the start and have made it better. Thanks for all you did to make this happen and keep it moving through an impossible timeline. Your understanding of integrity and wholeness made you guys the right publisher.

Thanks to Bill Dallas of CCN. Your heart for leaders is inspiring as you produce programs to help them thrive. Many are better because of you, and you model the concepts in this book.

Thanks to my students in the Masters of Organizational Leadership at Biola University. Your questions and class interactions have been helpful over the years as we walked through this material. Thanks also to Dr. Dan Maltby for the same.

Thanks to Bill Hybels and the Willow Creek Association for including me in your work with leaders. You live these concepts and help others to do the same. I am grateful for our friendship.

Thanks to Denis Beausejour, for all the interaction around this model of character. Your input and experience have added much, as has your personal passion for developing integrity.

Thanks to Greg Campbell for all of your input and discussions regarding leadership character, your help with this book, and also for our partnership. If the whole business world operated like you do, they would know why they are doing what they are doing, and they would do it better.

Thanks to Maureen Price for your leadership in making the Ultimate Leadership workshops thrive. Many leaders are better off because of all you do to make these principles come to life there.

Thanks to Dr. John Townsend for your friendship, character, partnership, and the many discussions and writing projects about character over the years. It has been a great journey.

Thanks also to the guys who are great sources of business input to me:

Toby Walker, Peter Ochs, Tony Thomopoulos, and Greg Campbell. You are always there with an answer.

........................

# preface

You have heard all your life that character counts. You have desired integrity in yourself and in the people with whom you work. You have felt its effects, suffered when it has not been present, and benefited when it has. You know that it is real.

But, often, we do not connect the dots with how integrity of character really works day to day, and how it affects our real results in the areas of life which matter to us most. We do not think that the way to more profits is a shift in our own character makeup, or if we do, we often do not know where to begin. Nor do we know sometimes how to make the personal shifts that will make our relationships more fruitful.

In this book, we will look at six areas of character that will do exactly that. They will bring you results that you have not been able to obtain. They will solve the persistent problems that seem to have turned into patterns over the years and have appeared to have no answer. Together, these character traits will enable your talents and abilities to bring you the results that you know you should be getting, but sometimes haven't. You will learn about the kind of character that:

1. Creates and maintains trust
2. Is able to see and face reality
3. Works in a way that brings results
4. Embraces negative realities and solves them
5. Causes growth and increase
6. Achieves transcendence and meaning in life

You will see how these character traits supercede gifts, talents, and ability, and how the ones who have them succeed, and the ones who don't, ultimately fail. And, the fun part will be finding that all of us can grow in all of these areas, and that the journey itself is of great value. So, join me in that journey, as we look at how *Integrity* is the courage to meet the demands of reality.

—Henry Cloud, Ph.D.
Los Angeles, CA
2005

# I

# INTRODUCTION

## Why Integrity Matters

# 1

## the three essentials

my friend, being the obsessive mother that she is, asked me for a favor. She and her husband have two boys, who at the time were nineteen and twenty-one, and at that point in life where they were staring adulthood right in the face. I think she wanted to make sure that it was not they who blinked, so she asked me to perform that kind of end-around move whereby you parent your kids secretly through someone else without their knowing what hit them.

We were having dinner one night when she said, "Would you take the boys out for lunch and talk to them about success? They have been asking a lot of questions about how some people become so successful, and how they make it 'big.' I thought you could help give them some guidance while they were in the asking mode."

"Hmm," I said, "probably not. That's really not my field, success.

I don't know much about it, so I wouldn't really know what to say. Why don't you call Zig Ziglar?" I was thinking about all of that literature with principles of success, how to make it big, how to reach the top, etc., and that was just not an area where I spent a lot of time. So, I politely declined, hoping a little humor would get her off this track.

"*Oh, come on,*" she protested. "They are twenty years old. You know enough to give them some things to think about. You have done a lot of things and worked with a lot of successful people. How hard can this be? Just take them out and tell them *something*. It doesn't have to be that perfect, just give them some things to think about. Push them a little in the right direction."

Feeling that I had been a little dismissive of the idea, I relented. "OK, I'll take them out and tell them something."

"Great! What will you tell them?" she immediately asked.

"I don't know. I'll have to think about it and come up with something."

"Yeah, but what do you think that will be?"

"I don't know," I repeated. "I'll think about it and give them something that will at least get them thinking."

"Yeah, but when you do think about it, what do you think it will be?"

I could see that this was a mother on a mission, and I was not getting off the hook. So, I thought for a moment about some really successful people that I know or have worked with and, off the top of my head, gave her an instant formulation for becoming a successful person or leader, while trying to remain true to my area of expertise as she was trying to morph me into a motivational speaker.

"OK, here is what I will tell them," I said. "People who become leaders, or really successful, tend to have three qualities. Number one, they have some set of competencies. In other words, they know their field, their industry, their discipline, or whatever. If you are Bill Gates, it helps to know something about the computer industry. If you are going to be a leading surgeon, you have to know what you are doing. In other words, *you can only fake it for so long, boys. So, get yourself in the library or wherever and master your craft.* Get good at what you do. A CEO has mastered a set of competencies in the same way. You just have to get good at what you do, period. There are no shortcuts.

"But," I continued in my miniseminar, "there are a lot of people who are competent and good at what they do who don't get to be leaders or 'hugely' successful. They do a good job, are happy and fulfilled, but they are not the ones that are catching your boys' attention. For someone to get to the level of accomplishment that they are asking about, he or she must possess the second ability. They have to be what I would call an alliance builder. In other words, they have to take their competencies and what they do well and build alliances with others who have competencies and resources and form relationships that are mutually beneficial. As a result, they leverage what they do well to much greater heights than just being 'good' at their job. They create alliances that make things a lot *bigger.* They forge relationships and partnerships with people like investors, regulators, distribution channels, their boards, city governments, Wall Street, or whoever it is that has the capacity to make what they are doing bigger.

"Even within a company, they have to form alliances with other parts of the company to be successful and move their agenda forward. Otherwise, they are just moving their little piece. There is nothing wrong with that, but again, people who make their 'piece' bigger always multiply it with things outside of themselves. They have to learn to build these alliances if they are going to be 'successful' in the way that they are talking about. If a person who leads sales can forge an alliance with the production group, he can get what he needs on time to satisfy the market. And, the production group can feel like their interests are met at the same time. Alliance building is key to success and leadership. It is more than 'networking,' which is often just a synonym for leeching. Alliances are about creating *leverage* to take what you do to a multiple.

"Now, having said that, let's get to the real issue that I would want to talk to them about. I would tell them that the people who possess the first two abilities are a dime a dozen. There is no shortage of talented, brainy people who are very, very good at what they do and are able to work the system and schmooze other people to get things done. There are zillions of them, and we all see them every day. But if your boys are truly going to make it, they have to have the third ingredient as well:

They have to have the character
to not screw it up.

"That is what I think I will tell them, if you have to know right now."

## The Character Problem: You've Seen It Happen

It took a little explaining to help her understand what I meant by "character," but when I talk about this issue in corporate settings, most people immediately get it when I ask this question: "How many of you have had a situation in your work experience where someone was very bright, talented, competent, and good at working deals, but there was something about who he or she was *as a person* that somehow got in the way of all of that ability?" At that point, people begin to roll their eyes, smile, look at each other knowingly, and do other things that show that we can all relate to this reality. At some level, we all know that "making it" involves more than talent or ability. It has something to do with personhood as well.

Then there is the more difficult question, and the one that gets to the point: "How many of you can also relate to there being some way in which *you* feel like if you were different in some way, that you could go further than you have or reach the full potential that your brains, talents, and competencies would allow?" I don't ask for hands, but from the nods and expressions, it is always clear that most of us can relate to this reality as well. "Making it" is more than just being competent and able to cut deals. It has a lot to do with who we are. But, exactly what does that mean? What *is* character? How does it affect performance? How important is it?

Most of the time, when we think of the word *integrity*, or *character*, we think of morals or ethics, not performance. We associate the topic with the catastrophes like Enron, Andersen, Worldcom, or the fall of individual superstars whose character has somehow gotten in the way. And certainly, there are those huge examples, from the top of business and government, all the way to the Church. There have been some huge ethical lapses that caused some major losses of not only individual careers, but entire companies and even confidence in the markets themselves. Not to mention the individuals who have been injured as well. Most people will now say "character counts." If they don't, they have been asleep for the last ten years.

But, when they say that, often what they mean is that *character is a "safeguard" against bad things happening.* In other words, if people have good character, their ethics and integrity will be such that you can truly trust the numbers, they won't steal from you, lie to you, cheat you, or be duplicitous. They can be trusted. You can sleep at night without watching your back. And, that kind of character is certainly bedrock, foundational, and without which we have nothing. As we have seen, when that is not there, everything can disappear. Morals and ethics undergird our entire system of business, relationships, government, finance, education, and even our very lives. Talk to any

wife or husband who has been cheated on, or any business partner
who has been lied to, and you will see what a relationship without
trust does to people.

However, that is not all of what I meant when I said that I
wanted to talk about character to those two boys, or to any of us either. Certainly, I wanted them to be honest, ethical, and not duplicitous. I wanted them to be trustworthy. I wanted them to be
faithful and dependable and have honor and be able to do the right
thing when no one is watching. But, I kind of assumed they did
those things, as I do of most of you who are reading this book. I assume that you know the importance of ethics and morals, of truth
and honesty. And I also know that under certain circumstances, living those out may even be hard for you, and in this book we will address that issue as well, such as when it gets difficult to be as ethical
or as honest as you want to be. But what I was really saying about
character was much more than trying to have a moral safeguard
against "getting into trouble."

What I was saying was this:


<u>who a person is</u>
will ultimately determine if their brains, talents,
competencies, energy, effort, deal-making abilities,
and opportunities will succeed.


It is one's makeup as a person, in ways much more than ethics
alone, that takes people to success or enables them to sustain it if
they ever achieve it. While character includes our usual understanding of ethics and integrity, it is much more than that as well.
Another way of putting it is that ethical functioning is a part of
character, but not all of it. And it certainly is not all of what affects
whether someone is successful or becomes a good leader.

In my own experience in over twenty years of working with CEOs, boards, managers, management teams, VPs, partners, supervisors, investors, and those who have a stake in their performance, I have seen many honest, ethical people of "integrity" who were not making it in some way. While we would say that they all were people of good "character," the reality is that their "personhood" was still preventing their talents and brains from accomplishing all that was in their potential. Some aspects to who they were as people that they had never seen as important to develop were keeping them from reaching the heights that all of the other investments they had made should have afforded them. While they met the criteria for having "integrity," they also left behind a trail of falling short in some key areas of performance that left them, as well as their stakeholders and the people who depend on them, wanting more. They were unable to successfully:

- Gain the complete trust of the people they were leading, and capture their full hearts and following.
- See all of the realities that were right in front of them. They had blind spots regarding themselves, others, or even the markets, customers, projects, opportunities, or other external realities that kept them from reaching their goals.
- Work in a way that actually produced the outcomes that they should have produced, given their abilities and resources.
- Deal with problem people, negative situations, obstacles, failures, setbacks, and losses.
- Create growth in their organization, their people, themselves, their profits, or their industry.
- Transcend their own interests and give themselves to larger purposes, thus becoming part of a larger mission.

These kinds of issues, as we shall see, have little to do with IQ, talent, brains, education, training, or most of the other important components of success. Instead, they have to do with the other aspects of character functioning that we pay way too little attention to in training people to be leaders and to be successful. *The most important tool ultimately is the person and his or her makeup, and yet it seems to get the least amount of attention and work.* Mostly, we focus on professional skills and knowledge instead.

For example, when in your business training or education did you ever take a course on "how to lose well"? I don't remember one. Yet, for example, I did a consulting project with an organization that lost millions and millions of dollars because the president was emotionally unable to "let go" of an agenda that was very, very dead. But because of his inability to "lose," and let it go, he took the company down a road to near disaster. He had a lot of integrity and would never have lied to anyone. But, he also could not face the reality of losing something he was very invested in, as all leaders must be able to do from time to time in order to regroup, recover, and succeed. That is about character.

My contention is that those kinds of character, or personal-makeup, issues have more to do with someone's ultimate ability than we give credit to. But, we don't get courses that teach us to develop those aspects of character. When we do, however, and begin to focus on them, then we see people begin to soar to the heights that their abilities should have been taking them all along.

You have seen the character problem and, if you are like most of us, have probably even lived it out to some degree yourself. You have experienced being on the other end of someone who needed to make some changes in these kinds of issues and have maybe even suffered the results of its not happening. But what you might not have seen, and what this book is about, is a way of thinking about what those issues are. We will look at a way of thinking about character and its components that if applied, can help you, those you work with, and your organization to avoid the three pitfalls that these issues cause:

1. Hitting a performance ceiling that is much lower than one's aptitude
2. Hitting an obstacle or situation that derails you
3. Reaching great success only to self-destruct and lose it all

In my experience in leadership and performance consulting, these are the three areas that character affects. Either someone is not reaching his full potential and is stuck at some level beneath his abilities, or some particular situation that he is not equipped to deal with does him in, or he does reach great heights and then something about his makeup brings him down. Most of the time, these three scenarios have little to do with competencies, brains, or talents, but everything to do with the person. Our goal is to understand what the issues are so that we can resolve them and their effect in your life. But to do that, we need to get a more complete view of character and how it affects your outcomes in life.

That is what I told my friend that I would tell the boys as she pressed me for an answer. Sometimes the things we say off the top of our head are the most true, as they come out of our experience more than out of our head. I think that is what happened that night, as I was not talking theory or academia. I was just telling her what I had seen from a lot of years of sitting and listening to talented people who for one reason or another were not getting to where their talents and potential should have been taking them. And, conversely, watching some world-class achievers do amazing things out of the character strengths that they possessed.

So, I will be sharing with you from that same place. I will not talk a lot about the leadership literature, or the success principles that you know well. This is not a book about casting vision or developing critical mass or how to become a change agent. Those are important parts to leadership and success, but tend to fall into the category of competencies, and you probably get a lot of training in those areas.

Instead, I will be sharing with you my experience from over twenty years of getting to work with people from all kinds of fields about the personal issues that keep some of them stuck and cause others to be amazing performers. It is my belief and experience that when people understand what these issues are and begin to grow in them, they are able to get to places they always thought possible, but could never quite attain.

# 2

## character, integrity, and reality

"**S**o what's the problem?" I asked the CEO. Usually when someone needs a consult, he does not begin with so many accolades about the "problem person." But Brad had done just that for the last ten minutes. He had told me how "incredible" and "brilliant" Rick, his VP of sales, was, and how the numbers had increased so dramatically since he'd joined the company a couple of years before. It was almost as if he were selling me on his abilities more than asking for my help with a problem. "It sounds like he is doing an incredible job. What is it that you are struggling with?"

"Well, as good as the numbers are, I have two key people who are about to leave if I don't get rid of him. They have told me that I have to choose either them or him. I don't want to do that. I need his performance and abilities. He really is amazing at what he does

well, but, there are some 'issues' on the people side. The rest of the
team has gotten divided when it comes to him too. Some of them
want him to be here because of the sheer performance. They like
the horsepower.

"But, other people really don't like him. We had one case where
a woman brought a case against us for what she termed 'harass-
ment,' and we just settled it. I don't think it was that big a deal, but
she obviously did, and in the end that was what mattered. If you ask
me, he is not a bad guy. He just is run and gun and drives people
pretty hard, and a strong personality. Some of the people who don't
have the gut for that end up feeling like he is running over them, or
not giving them the respect they feel like they deserve. So, they get
upset. I don't want to lose him, though. He is too valuable. But, I
have to do something and I was hoping you could get the team back
together, or fix him, or something. Whatever. But we need something."

I could almost feel the desperation that he felt, as if a big part of
his world depended on finding a solution to his top performer's
"people issues."

"How do you feel about him?" I asked.

"Well, obviously I am for him. I mean, look at the numbers.
They speak for themselves, and if you talk to him about any of this,
that is what he will say as well. It is hard to tell him that he is a problem when he can just point to how well we are doing. And, that is a
little of where I find myself too. I don't mind him, and he is getting
us to places where we couldn't have gotten to without him. So, he is
helping me."

"So you think his 'numbers' are what the revenues show? That is
how you come up with thinking he is a good deal?" I asked. "By the
sales figures?"

"Well, yes. That is his job, to make the revenue side work."

"But what about the expense side?"

"That's not his job. Our CFO, controller, project managers, and others watch the expenses."

"I didn't mean watching the expenses," I said. "I meant the expense side of having him here."

"You mean his compensation? He is compensated well, but he is more than worth it. He brings in a lot more than his compensation package," the CEO explained, probably thinking that I was just not getting it that the guy's sales numbers were much more than enough to pay for him.

"No, that is not what I meant by expense. What I meant were the other expenses that he creates. Let me list a few:

- If you take what the company pays you as CEO, including your options, and put an hourly rate on that, it is a huge number. How many hours do you think you have spent listening to other people talk about their problems with him over the past couple of years? Just a few meetings a week would get us in the hundreds of hours. Multiply that times your hourly rate to the company and you get a different picture of his expense to you.
- To that number add the amount the hours are worth of the people who were spending time talking to you instead of doing their jobs.
- To that number, add the lost opportunity of what you and your people could have done in that time had you not been working out the problems regarding him.
- To that, add the amount of the settlement, and all of the hourly charges by the attorneys for the consults that you and your HR people have had about this problem.
- To that add the cost of finding two new VPs to replace the two that are about to leave, and the lost business, work, and traction in that time lag.

● To that, add the distraction that this whole problem becomes from the morale and direction of the company and what it is trying to do.

"Now you are getting a better picture of his expense. Do you still feel like he is such a great deal?" I asked.

"Well, not when you put it like that," he said, looking a little sheepish, as if he had been caught not watching his wallet and was embarrassed that he had been robbed. "Not when you put it like that."

## The Wake

I went on to talk to Brad about a concept that I call the wake. One of my favorite things to do is to sit on the aft deck of a boat going across the ocean and just watch the wake. It is such a beautiful, ever-changing creation as the ship continues on its path. You can tell a lot about a ship as you look at its wake.

If it is in a straight line, you get a feeling that the boat is steadily on course, and that the captain is not dozing at the wheel, or that an engine or a shaft is not somehow out of whack. But if it is wavering, you begin to wonder. Also, if it is smooth and flat, you know something about the speed of the boat, and if it is steep, you can tell something about its drag. In other words, what the wake looks like can tell you a lot about the boat itself.

With people, the same thing is true. As a person goes through a company, like Brad's sales guy, *he or she leaves a wake behind as well.* And just as with a boat, there are always two sides to the wake that a leader or someone else leaves when moving through our lives or the life of an organization. The two sides of the wake are:

1. The task
2. The relationships

When a person travels through a few years with an organization, or with a partnership, or any other kind of working association, he leaves a "wake" behind in these two areas, *task* and *relationship:* **What did he accomplish and how did he deal with people?** And we can tell a lot about that person from the nature of the wake.

In terms of the task, what does the wake look like? Is it a wake of goals being reached? Profits being made? Growth of the business or the deal that the person was working on with you? The mission being accomplished? Things getting completed? New ways of doing things being introduced and perfected? A stronger brand? A stronger reputation for the work and company? Better systems and processes? Cleaner operations?

Or, is it a different kind of wake? Unreached goals and projections? Misfires? Mission not accomplished? Lack of completion? Disorganization and chaos? Inactivity and nothing happening? Lack of focus? False starts? Resources and money lost?

And from the wake, which is the real performance and results, we can tell a lot about the person. Results *matter.* They are the stuff from which we are evaluated and for which we strive to bring our dreams and plans into reality. When we look at results, the wake, we are really looking at *ourselves* and learning something about our character in the same way that the wake of a ship tells us a lot about the ship.

At the end of the day, we must look back and see if the wake of our work is profitable or not. If it isn't, it is time to ask ourselves some hard questions. The wake is the results we leave behind. *And the wake doesn't lie and it doesn't care about excuses.* It is what it is. No matter what we try to do to explain why, or to justify what the wake is, it still remains. It is what we leave behind and is our record.

On the other side of the wake are the relationships. Just as we leave the effects of our work behind in results, we leave the effects of our interactions with people behind in their hearts, minds, and souls. We leave a wake of people behind us as we move through their lives and their organizations. We leave a wake behind as we move through the lives of clients and partners. We leave a wake behind as we move through our relationships with vendors and other alliances, as well as our entire industry. So, we must look out over the transom and ask ourselves, "What does that wake look like?"

Are a lot of people out there water-skiing on the wake, smiling, having a great time for our having "moved through their lives"? Or are they out there bobbing for air, bleeding, and left wounded as shark bait? In other words, would they say that their experience with us has left them better off for our having "moved through their lives," or would they say that it has left them worse off? Did they consider it a blessing that they were associated with you, or a curse? What is the nature of the wake? Are they smiling or reeling?

In the people side, just as in the task side, there are results. Are they more trusting after working with us? Are they more fulfilled as people? Have they grown as a result of being associated with you? Do they feel better about themselves, and working with others? Did they learn from you and feel lifted up and encouraged? Were they stretched and inspired to become more than they were before they worked with or for you? Did your relationship cause them to produce more?

Or, are they wounded? Less trusting? Feeling put down, cheated, or manipulated? Disappointed, let down, or lied to? Are they angry and just waiting for a chance to get even? Do they feel inferior, like a loser, or ashamed because of how you interacted with them? And the big question: "Would they want to do it again?"

Recently I hired someone in an important position. In doing all of the due diligence in my search, I called two of her former bosses. I asked a lot about the wake on both sides, the task side and the relationship side. It was encouraging to hear them talk about her work, the results that she would always get, and the way that people who worked with her and clients felt about her. I also pushed and asked about the downsides of the wake as well. They told me a few things about her that were ripples in the wake, i.e., ways that she could improve. I paid attention to them, as I knew that if I hired her, I would also run into those aspects of her wake as well. In my estimation, as in theirs, these were not a big deal.

But, then I asked both of them the big question: *"Would you do it again?"* Before I got the question out of my mouth, one said, "In a heartbeat." The other blurted out, "Absolutely." No hesitation. *That was the answer that I needed,* for it was clearly out of the wake that she had left behind. Since I know that those kinds of wakes are produced out of who a person is, I could be confident in the kind that she is most likely to leave with me.

So, that is how I wanted Brad to evaluate his VP. Look at the total *reality* of the wake. The truth is that his character, who he was as a person, was leaving a wake behind that included much more than just the sales numbers. Upon first glance, his "task" wake looked good, until you began to see all of the other things that he was leaving in that wake that were getting in the way of the task itself, e.g., getting people in high-leverage positions sidetracked, taking time away from the CEO's focus and duties, using resources to solve problems that he was causing, and potentially causing a serious hole in the upper-management team. These are all things that affect the task, the mission, and the bottom line. We are not talking just about being "nice." We are talking about real results, results that come from character.

And, on the pure relationship side of things, people were definitely not water-skiing on the wake of working with him. Some were headed to the emergency room, and others were just hating the climate that he was developing. In just about every direction, things did not look good, and even with the people who were not negative on him, such as the CEO, it was because they were just looking at shortsighted results and not at the larger cancer that was growing right in front of them.

In the end, the CEO was slow to do what he should have done, and the board got involved. The superstar was disciplined for some things and left, with a hefty severance. The CEO left shortly thereafter as a result of losing the confidence of the board. Not a healthy wake for either of them as we look back. And the sad thing is that it was not a "business" problem. It was not a "competency" problem. It was not a "talent" problem, a "brains" problem, or a shortfall in "deal-making." Neither the CEO nor the sales guy lacked any of those qualities or abilities. They were gifted people. But they did have some shortfalls in the thing that leaves the wake: **character**.

> The problems that the sales guy caused, and the
> problems that the CEO had in dealing with those
> problems, were results of their individual makeups
> that manifested themselves in a wake of failure.

In the case of the sales VP, his relational abilities left a lot to be desired. His interpersonal dealings not only left people being hurt by working with him, and disliking him, but also desiring to leave the company as a result of having to work with or report to him. Not a good wake on that side of the boat. And, on the task side, although he appeared to be doing well, his *interpersonal shortcomings got in the way so much that the very tasks that he was accomplishing were getting compromised in a big way and ultimately brought down to nothing.* All because of some character issues and none because of "business" issues.

And we can say the same thing for the CEO. He was smart and gifted as well, but who he was as a *person allowed* this VP to virtually split his company apart and cause things to fragment to such a degree that key people were either completely disrupted or looking at leaving. His inability to deal with the relational side of his work eventually caused the task side of things to go down as well. In effect, due to his personal weaknesses, he lost everything he had worked for. Not a good wake, and all because of this thing called "character."

## A Different Definition of Character

As I said in the first chapter, when we think of things like character or integrity, we often think of matters related to morals and ethics. We want to know that someone is "trustworthy" or "faithful." We want to be able not to have to audit their numbers. And if those things are in place, then we often put the character issue to rest and begin to talk about business or performance abilities, competencies, and the like.

Yet, when you look at the real world, *there are dimensions to a person's makeup that deeply affect the results, the wake, that they leave behind that definitely are germane to the task* and yet often do not get the focus that they deserve. Take Brad's sales VP, for example. Do you think that anyone ever asked him in his job interview how he goes about building trust with people and making sure that other parts of the company trust him as well? But he obviously lacked that interpersonal ability, and it made all of his strategic initiatives that were extremely effective worthless in the end. Ultimately, it turned out to be the most important thing.

Similarly, in his interview or training, how much attention do you think was paid to his ability to regain broken trust or repair a relationship after a conflict? Or to making other team members feel valued and want to give all of their service to him? Obviously not enough, nor does it appear that he paid much attention to developing those aspects of his personhood either. In the end, it cost him and the company dearly. We can see that even though those two skills were *relational* in nature, they affected both the relational and the task side of the wake.

And, the truth is that those issues flowed out from who he was as a person, his makeup. That is what I am referring to as character that includes more than ethics and morals. Similarly, Brad, the CEO, had his own character or makeup issues that affected his own wake as well. Do you think it was a lack of business sense in Brad that created this mess? Certainly not. He understood the markets, the strategies, the operations, and the other aspects of the business picture. He also understood that he had a problem with Brad. All of those calls with the attorneys kind of clued him in on that reality. But, in the end, it was something about his makeup that kept him from dealing with this issue directly.

The reality was that he allowed himself, *out of a state of need, to become too dependent on this VP's performance and was afraid to deal with the issue head-on.* He was afraid of losing him, and losing the performance. He was also afraid of confronting in a direct way someone that he needed so much. He just couldn't bring himself to doing the hard confrontations that were needed. He could not get tough enough to face into it. Instead, he avoided the conflict and tried to placate the other members of the management team into feeling as if things were really OK when they weren't. In the end, he lost them.

But both Brad and his VP were men of "character" in that they never lied to anyone or cheated anyone or did any shady dealings. Both were impeccably responsible. Both were dependable with regard to anyone's code of ethics. But, they both had what I would call "character" issues that led to their performance problems. So, that leaves us with a need for a definition of "character" to work with as we take a look at the issues that affect performance.

## Character, Makeup, and Ability

Let me explain with an analogy. If you are a general in the air force, and you need a new airplane built, you go see Boeing or someone like them and tell them that you want a new jet. They get a roomful of engineers together, and before they decide on what kind of material, or metal, they will use to build the airplane, they have to ask you an important question: What are you going to do with this plane?

If you say you want it to be able to go from a standstill to 600 mph in a flash, then they will design it in one way. They think, "The character of that design will not withstand that kind of torque. It will begin to break apart at that kind of acceleration. We need a design with a different character, or makeup."

If you say the plane is going to have to perform at forty thousand feet, then dip down to the desert and withstand certain heat, or later that day fly over the north pole under radar and withstand certain cold temperatures, they begin to look at other kinds of metal with a different character as well. They are thinking about the design's character. If it has to carry cargo or reach other speeds or go for long distances without refueling and thus have better fuel efficiency, then weight and other issues begin to get specifically important. If the flight patterns are going to have incredible demands on maneuverability with high speeds, the "integrity" of the material has to be of a certain kind so as to not come apart with those tricky moves. Character is *everything, depending on what demands are going to be put upon the design.*

In the same way that the realities of torque, weather, temperature, gravity, and other things put demands on a metal that it has to meet in order to perform and not crash, there are *realities that put demands on people that they have to meet in order to perform and not crash as well.*

And the character of the person is what determines his or her ability to meet those reality demands, i.e., demands encountered in the real world. Thus, the definition that I will be working from for the purposes of this book is this:

> Character = the ability to meet the
> demands of reality.

In business and in all of life, reality demands come across one's path. And just as the "character" of the metal determines whether that airplane is going to succeed in that kind of heat or torque, a person's character determines whether he or she will succeed in that situation. Their makeup, their integrity, will either be able to deliver or not. They will meet the demand, and succeed, leaving a wake of goals being reached and people being fulfilled only if their character can meet that demand.

The demands that reality brings are many and varied. There are interpersonal demands, such as difficult people and relationships that one must negotiate and make work. Everyone, at whatever level of business he or she has conducted, has experienced that reality. The homeowner walks away from a remodel wondering, "Would this have turned out better if I could have dealt with that contractor differently?" The parent walks away from the teacher conference wondering, "Would my child have a better chance if I could deal with that teacher in a better way?" The boss walks through the corridor wondering, "Would we be getting better results if I could deal with that person's issues more effectively?" And everyone has wondered, "Would I be doing better if I could just somehow make it work better with my boss?" And there is always the reality of getting people or a team of people to trust you enough to make it all come together.

On the task side, the reality demands are ever present also.

Think of the realities that make demands on the metal of your character: You have put your lifeblood into a project for months, you get the first numbers back, and they are bad. What happens inside? Some people proactively wrap their arms around the situation, get energized, become clearheaded, get to work, and have all their capacities available to them. They turn it around. They meet the demand of the reality of bad numbers staring them in the face. They deliver. But other people go into a black hole, feel like a loser, get afraid, get mean, panic, stall out, or retreat. The bad numbers do them in.

Here is another example: You are given a new opportunity, project, or task. The possibilities are enormous. But, they bring realities that make tough demands. There is going to be a season of no rewards, and people are going to question your every decision to go in that direction. There is going to be risk, and the possibility of failure means a lot of loss. There are going to be chances to move too quickly as well. There is going to be the need to hold yourself back and be strategic before making a move, and then to have the courage to make it. You must be able to delay gratification and keep going while it is all building. What if a new opportunity comes along in the middle of things that looks attractive, but would sidetrack you and get you scattered? Can you say no to that one? Do you have the guts to eliminate the ones that are already distracting you? What if there are people involved that you need to move or lay off? What if you have to call the investors or the bank and ask them for more money? How is your "stomach" for those tasks?

Depending on your makeup, when those demands come, you will either meet their requirements and succeed, leaving a wake of results, or your makeup will be overcome by them. For some, opportunity itself causes a problem. The risk is too scary, the pressure too great, and fear overcomes talent, brains, and abilities. The status quo is more comfortable, yet not really. Or, you get too frustrated with the process, begin to take shortcuts, and screw it up in some way. *In the end, character always rules.*

In my experience as a leadership consultant, these kinds of personal issues make the difference in the ones who do well and the ones who don't. When I was discussing this book with someone whose husband is the CEO of a huge public corporation, she said, "This is so important. It is never the business issues that cause David stress. He loves those. It is always a problem that was caused by a *person. It is always the personal side that creates the problems, the stress, or messes up the goals.*" That is about someone who deals with billions of dollars and yet sees the character issues as the real stressors.

So my goal in this book is to take a look at those "personal issues" that make people successful or keep them from getting there. I have had the privilege of working with and consulting with some very successful people over the years, and there are reasons that they make it as they do, from Fortune 25 to family-held firms. I have gotten to watch them and see their character deliver results time and time again.

And as a consultant, I have seen the problems that these personal, character issues bring as well, even in people with enormous brains and talent. What I want to do here is to get specific about what those elements of character are that make it all go one way or the other, and in doing so, to give you a helpful template by which to grow into the person who can deliver whatever reality asks you to do. When you do that, *your brains, talents, and potential will intersect with reality and find themselves creating a wake that will be fulfilling to you, and enjoyable and profitable for those who are in it with you.*

And I want to give you hope for yourself, or for some of the ones that you work with or are responsible for. As we shall see, character can change and grow. That is the exciting part. The things that have held you back thus far from being whom you are designed to be do not have to continue to be your downfall, or "slowdown." Once you can see what they are, you can change them.

But, unfortunately, many people have been taught that it can't happen, and that is disappointing whenever I hear it. Just recently I talked to a young man who is graduating from one of the top business schools in the country, and he said as a result of his leadership courses that he had learned that "character doesn't change. You have to make sure you pick people with good character because that is what you are going to be stuck with. Character is fixed from early on." I almost came out of my chair, because nothing could be further from the truth. People grow and people change when the right experiences are brought to the person, and they have the right response in using those experiences.

Yes, character is "fixed," in that it is a *structure* like a house. Once you build it, it is pretty much going to stand there just like that. But, it is also true that just because it is "fixed" doesn't mean that you can't go in and start knocking down walls and adding others so that it becomes "fixed" in a different way. Those are two different issues. Just because something is an enduring structure doesn't mean that it is unchangeable. It all depends on what kinds of investment one is willing to make in bringing about that change, and whether it is worth it to the parties involved.

So, I agreed with him in a different way. You should *always* pick people with the best character possible, because of the very things I have been saying. It is what produces the results that you are looking for, and why in the world would you intentionally pick someone who is not equipped to deliver? Or that you would have to change or fix? But, selection and growth are two different issues. Hire and choose to work with the best, but don't ever forget that all of us can always change and be better. So, since you do have a big stake in your own success and results, you will be willing to make the investment that brings about change, no matter where you need to grow. As well as to help the ones you work with and depend on. That is the hope that you can have. I have seen it a zillion times.

But to grow, we have to know what character is, what it looks like, and ultimately what its relationship is to reality. Where does it intersect real life? That is the question that we will address.

## integrity

"Why don't you do what a lot of those rich guys do who are at your level of wealth?" I asked my friend. "They start buying sports teams, or airlines, and things like that."

"Because I don't know anything about those businesses," he said. "My own business is really all I know at very significant levels. So, I don't try to get into businesses that I don't understand."

"But, that's not true," I said. "I know of other businesses that you invest in. You have told me about some."

"No, that is not right. I never invest in businesses other than my own."

"But what about . . ." and I went on to list about five that I knew of that he had big investments in.

"I did not invest in those *businesses*. I invested in the *people*. I never invest in businesses I don't know anything about, but I will invest in a *person*. If I know their character, their history, how they operate, what kind of judgment they have, what kind of risks are acceptable to them, how they execute, and things like that, and I know them *well*, I will invest. But I don't go buy businesses I don't know anything about."

We were driving to an event, and when he said that, I think it was several miles before I said anything else. All I could do was reflect on what he had said. It was such a clear picture of what makes for success. It is not always the "market" or the "strategy" or the "resources." It is the *people*. When you have the right people on board, they deal with bad markets well. They come up with a way to make it work. When they get far enough along to find out that their strategy is flawed, or not working, they adapt and fix it. When they run out of resources, they either find out where they are losing them, or they find new ones. But, if you don't have the people he was talking about, then you can lose in a great market with a great strategy and a ton of resources.

What he was describing was a picture of character at work. But it was a particular kind of character. It was a character with "integrity." What is "integrity"? As I mentioned in chapter 1, when asked about integrity, we usually think of the moral and ethical aspects of integrity. And it is always absolutely essential that those things be present. As we shall see in the section on transcendence, without those aspects of integrity where someone can be depended on to live out values, everything falls apart. The structure of life, from relationships to societies, depends on moral and ethical structure being intact and practiced.

But, my friend was talking about more than that. He was talking about a complete picture of performance, all the way from gaining trust, to getting results, and a return on investment. And that is the way that we must think about "integrity" as well, if we are going to see results in any aspect of life.

Integrity is character, ethics, and morals. But it is also more, as even the *Oxford Dictionary* and the history of the word *integrity* itself tells us. Listen to the definitions as *Oxford Dictionary* (or whoever) lists them:

1. The quality of being honest and having strong moral principles; moral uprightness. "He is known to be a man of integrity."

(This is the first aspect we talk about and need when thinking of character. But, there is more.)

2. The state of being *whole* and *undivided:* "upholding territorial integrity and national sovereignty."
3. The condition of bring *unified, unimpaired,* or *sound in construction.* "The structural integrity of the novel."
4. *Internal consistency* or *lack of corruption* in electronic data.

And, the origins of the word we can see in the French and Latin meanings of *intact, integrate, integral,* and *entirety.* The concept means that the "whole thing is working well, undivided, integrated, intact, and uncorrupted." When we are talking about integrity, we are talking about being a whole person, an integrated person, with all of our different parts working well and delivering the functions that they were designed to deliver. It is about *wholeness* and *effectiveness* as people. It truly is "running on all cylinders."

That is what my friend was talking about. He would give millions only to a person who did not have a gaping hole in one side of the boat. It would not be enough for someone to be able to sell well, to have a good idea or a good business plan. For someone to get his money, the person would have to have good judgment as well. It would not be enough to be aggressive, or a risk taker. The person

would have to be able to finish things and be a closer, not leaving a
bunch of good ideas undone, unexecuted, and scattered. He would
have to know that the person had a "good wake," and that comes
from having a *complete* toolbox.

## Too Much to Ask?

It would be natural to begin to ask at this point, "What are you saying? That for someone to be successful that they have to be able
to do *everything* well? No one does everything well. We all have
strengths and weaknesses." And that is right. In fact, a lot of research and experience shows us that capitalizing on our strong
areas and avoiding our weak areas is an essential concept. Anyone
who thinks that a visionary, for example, should be doing the detail
of spreadsheets doesn't understand giftedness. First of all, it would
be a waste if George Lucas spent all of his time calling on and selling
films to distributors. Or if Tiger Woods had to negotiate and follow up with Nike. I am sure that if Tiger were a weak negotiator or
business executive, he could still win the Masters. And, more to the
point, if he were trying to be some "whole person" defined by having to do it all, then he would probably *not* win the Masters, as he
would be misusing his talents, spending time doing something he
might not do well and not doing what only he can do. If I am an investor, I want Tiger focusing on golf, not business.

So that is not the idea here. We all have strengths and weaknesses
and we need to operate in those strong areas where we are talented
and gifted. The idea here is about character that seems to *transcend*
gifts, talents, and other ways of thinking about "strengths." The
things we are going to look at, Tiger needs to have all of them, or the
lack of any one of them will begin to affect his career. As we shall see,
they are things that will actually affect the golf itself, whether or not
he ever decides to do the bookkeeping or selling of his name, brand,

image, products, and the like. And that is true of his accountant and business manager as well as whoever does all of the other functions in his kingdom. Bottom line: *the character issues will affect the one or two things you do well, forgetting any need to do the rest.*

> Another way of saying this is that while you
> don't need all the gifts that exist in the world,
> you do need all the aspects of character while
> you are putting your gifts to work.

For example, we will see that one aspect of character is almost purely "relational" in nature. And we could say that there are people who are "gifted in relational ways," and that they should focus in an area that uses those gifts. Put them in human resources or psychology or customer service. But as we saw in the last chapter, the VP of sales needs the relational abilities of character even if he doesn't need to have the "giftedness" for a people-oriented position. But, even the ones in the "people-oriented jobs" will fail if they do not have other character abilities, such as the ability to be in touch with the truth of a situation and to see it clearly (another character dimension we will look at). If they lack that ability that is not so relational in nature, then their living out of their *gifted* area is going to suffer greatly. Character transcends gifts and the context of the expression of those gifts.

So, the concept of integrity being about needing *wholeness* in all areas of character does not negate the reality that we are not gifted in all areas, nor the reality that we do best when we are working within our gifts. What it does say is that if we do not have integrity of character, wholeness of character functioning in the ways that we will describe it, *then our ability to capitalize on our strengths will be severely affected.* In the last chapter, there is no doubt that Rick was working in his area of giftedness, which was sales. But, a lack of wholeness in

character integrity, not his gifted area, did him in. We need our
gifts, but without wholeness of character—integrity as we are calling it—our gifts will become unusable or at least less fruitful. You
can be the best designer in the world, but if no one will talk to you,
or you can't complete a proposal on time, you will be designing the
inside of Dumpsters. You still have to be able to "deliver the goods"
no matter what your level of giftedness. So, let's see what this character looks like that is able to deliver the goods, to "meet the demands of reality," or, to be a person of "integrity."

## Character That Delivers in the Real World

What is wholeness? There are a lot of ways to look at it and a lot of
definitions. I in no way think mine to be the "right" one. What I
have tried to do is to take the dimensions of character functioning
that I have seen affect people's effectiveness the most and put them
into a model that will help us look at ourselves and grow. I can as-
sure you that many other good models about character and integrity are out there. What this one attempts to do is to share the
most discrete aspects of character functioning that affect results.
The bulk of my work with leaders has been when there is some sort
of breakdown in *results:* results with the task or mission, and/or results with the people. And as we have seen in the case of Brad and
Rick, results in the interaction of the two.

   What I have tried to do here is to take those aspects of character
and put them into functions that tend to be different from each
other, therefore discrete, and at the same time, related to each
other, therefore integrated. If we have that combination, then we
can focus on specific *aspects* of our makeup and, at the same time,
be focusing on *all* of our makeup and getting it working together.
That is what brings results and effectiveness, i.e., when we can
focus enough on specific issues to grow and as a result, get it all

working together. Let's now look at what those aspects of character are:

1. The ability to connect authentically (which leads to trust)
2. The ability to be oriented toward the truth (which leads
   to finding and operating in reality)
3. The ability to work in a way that gets results and finishes
   well (which leads to reaching goals, profits, or the mission)
4. The ability to embrace, engage, and deal with the negative
   (which leads to ending problems, resolving them, or
   transforming them)
5. The ability to be oriented toward growth (which leads to
   increase)
6. The ability to be transcendent (which leads to enlarge-
   ment of the bigger picture and oneself)

*If people are able to function well in these areas, the good wake is virtually in-
evitable.* Their gifts are able to come to fruition in the real world and
get real results for meaningful purposes. And the people with
whom they accomplish those, as well as the people for whom they
accomplish those goals, are better off for having been with them.
Likewise, the ways in which we are incomplete in these things will
have a real effect on our fruitfulness both functionally as well as relationally. We will see it in the wake.

At this point in our discussion, it will be difficult to completely
see what I am referring to with regards to what all of these actually
mean. But if you just take a cursory view of them, you can see why
seeing "integrity" as "integration of all the parts" is key, and why
when we are not intact as a person, meaning that one or more of
these areas is underdeveloped, amiss, or otherwise unavailable, we
get into trouble.

What if, for example, someone is good at the fourth trait, the ability to face negative realities and solve them. She would be a good problem solver. But, let's say that she was lacking in the fifth quality and had little orientation toward creating growth. She would end up being a "maintainer," fixing things that were broken or were problems, but not making any of the existing good things bigger, or expanding into new areas either. Over time, and not much time, she would flatline, and we know what happens to any business or organization or person that has flatlined and stopped growing: they are usually going backward and the indicators have just not caught up yet. They are often dying if they are not growing. A flat line is usually the beginning of a downward line.

Or, as I hinted at earlier, what if someone is really good at building connections, establishing trust with people, and treating them in ways that strengthen the bonds. But, there is a real weakness in their orientation toward the truth and they have blind spots that keep them out of touch with certain realities. Then, they end up forging connections with people or in situations where real warning signs are telling them to back off, not go forward. They do not see what is wrong with someone or a situation. There are going to be some real effects in their decision-making, alliances, ability to deal with the resulting problems, and ultimately the fruits of it all. The street term for this is *he is just too trusting*. But, it comes from a lack of other parts being integrated into trust so that the trust ability is pure and not corrupted.

There are many other examples that a lack of integration of character brings about and we shall see, but suffice it to say at this point that integration or incompleteness in these areas of functioning is a huge problem with real-life results, both personally and professionally for people. The reason is that the opposite of integration is *compartmentalization*. That means that a part of oneself can be operating without the benefit of other parts, and that spells trouble.

You have known people who love, for example, without the benefit of judgment and reality testing. Or people who are creative, but without the benefit of being structured or organized. Or those who can be proactive and take risks, but can't delay when they need to. They are impulsive. *Strengths turn into weaknesses without the other parts of a person to balance them out.* In fact, historically the word *diabolical* actually means "to compartmentalize." Things go "bad" when they are out of balance and integration. The person of "integrity" is a person of balanced integration of all that character affords.

## The Gap

Besides integration, or completeness, there is also the problem of underdevelopment in these areas, which we will focus on in great detail throughout the book. What happens when we are underdeveloped in one of these critical areas? First of all, it means we are human. That is the good news! The nature of the human race is that we never get to "completeness" or "maturity" in the fullest sense of the word. There is always room for improvement. There is the "gap" between where we are at any given moment, the true reality, and the ideal of the construct itself, ultimate reality. So, don't be too hard on yourself.

If you take any of the six character traits, we can conceive of what it would be, or at least think about what it would be, to be perfect in that ability. A "flawless" connector, or problem solver. But, the reality is that none of us is there. We are somewhere on a continuum from little ability to connect and the ideal. So, underdevelopment leaves a gap between where we are at any given moment and where we need to be. **That gap is our need and opportunity for growth.**

It is also the place where dysfunction occurs and the interruptions in our pursuits of goals and relationships. Remember, character equals the ability to meet the demands of reality. So, to reach our goals and deliver in our relationships, we have to be able to negotiate those realities or they crush us, stop us, hurt us, or thwart us. The places at which we are *underdeveloped* are the places at which problems occur. If you remember, in chapter 1, I talked about three specific ways in which this occurs:

1. Hitting a performance ceiling that is much lower than one's aptitude
2. Hitting an obstacle or situation that derails you
3. Reaching great success only to self-destruct and lose it all

Character growth is what insures us that these three things will not happen or will happen in lessening degrees over time.

Besides our just not closing the gap between where we are and where we should be, a bigger problem can occur when we lack character integrity. The bigger problem is that we become "dysfunctional" in the truest sense of the word. With all the talk in the last years about dysfunctional families, management teams, people, and the like, it might be good to define what I mean by the term.

I do not mean *imperfection,* or that you make mistakes, or that you have areas of immaturity, weaknesses, or flaws. Those things just mean that you are human. That is the "gap." Imperfection is normal, expected, and even exciting and fun to deal with and work on. Getting better and growing is fun. What I mean by *dysfunctional* is something way worse than the natural need to be or do better.

*Dysfunctional* as I use it means that not only is someone imperfect in some ability, but the *actual exertion of effort in that area causes more problems, or a greater gap, than it solves.* In other words, it would have been better if people had not tried, because the end result is worse than where they started.

You have probably worked with someone who, when he would

not show up for work, allowed the team or company to be better off and get more done. You could accomplish more when he was absent than when trying to contribute. Or, the person who tries to resolve a conflict with someone, but only makes it worse. In the attempt at resolution, these people not only repeat the original mistakes, but add some new ones as well. They go in to apologize for something and end up yelling at the other person or blaming him or her in the apology. It would have been better for them not to have shown up at all.

It is the old problem of trying to wipe off the windshield, but the rag is greasy, and every effort leaves a smudge. In these cases, it would be better if someone just sat on his hands and did nothing. That is what dysfunction is: when an effort toward making something better makes it worse. That is when we are in trouble. And both a lack of integration and a lack of development can do that.

## Moving to Greater Realities: The Necessity for Growth in Integrity

What have we seen so far? First, there is more to being successful in one's pursuits of goals and in one's relationships than being competent and able to build alliances and networks. Character makes it all work in the end, and character is defined as the ability to meet the demands of reality.

Second, character has components to it, or traits, and areas of functioning where it operates. Those contexts are the real places where our personhood and reality interface and results occur, either positive or negative.

Third, past character traits, we need character "integration," or "integrity." That is the "condition of being *unified, unimpaired,* or *sound in construction,*" as the *Oxford Dictionary* puts it. Just think what it would be like if you were unified, or "at one with" all of your abilities and potentials. What could stop you? Then, you would truly be "unimpaired," and no weakness or obstacle could slow you down or hold you back. You would be so "sound in construction" that the purposes for which the "metal" was designed would actually be accomplished. You would truly meet the demands that any reality threw at you and be fruitful in the end. Any tough relationship issue that came your way, you would be able to solve. Any tough business reality or complex situation, you would negotiate to its knees. Since you were still human, you might not do it perfectly. But, you would do it effectively and fruitfully as the process went on.

So, that gives us the vision for our journey through this look at integrity. The way that I see it, it is threefold:

1. To see the nature of reality results, fruitfulness, and success. This means to face up to the fact that the nature of reality is that we can only deal with it to the level of our integrity of character. There are no shortcuts, tricks, "fooling it," or any other way to be successful if we do not possess the stuff that each situation is demanding from us. We must bend the knee to the necessity for personal development. To the degree that we do that, we are getting closer to whatever our goal is. To the degree that we avoid it, we are getting further away.

2. To understand the components of character itself. To diagnose a problem is a lot of the cure. To understand what the real issue is leads us to knowing what to do. As we take a hard look at dissecting the six areas of character into what makes them work, we will know what to focus on in our personal development. We will be able to see exactly what issue is holding us back, and to put our arms around it and begin to grow.

3. To work toward a full integration of character and wholeness as a person. Instead of compensating for incomplete-

ness by asking our areas of strength to do things they were not designed to do, we can begin to gain the strength that real integrity provides: no cracks in the armor. As we integrate and become whole, each time we take a step, there is no dysfunction that makes us end up two steps back. Integration brings the greatest amount of fulfillment for everyone concerned, and the greatest wake wherever we go.

## What Kind of Force?

One of the words that is close to character or integrity in meaning is the Hebrew word that is translated "virtue." If you trace its origins and meanings, one of the meanings is a "force." Someone of virtue is a force, and a force always leaves a result. When a hurricane comes through a town, you can see the results of its force. When the wind moves across the water, or through the trees, you can see the results of its force.

Likewise, when you move through life, through your company or organization, through your career, and through your relationships, your character is going to be a "force." The question is, "What kind of force is it going to be?" Will it be one of virtue, where you deliver the goods? When you bring energy and force of character to a goal or a project, will the force bring about fruit? When you bring energy and force to a relationship, will there be a good result? In many ways, as we shall see, it is up to you. That is good news. So, the goal here is to develop these aspects of character that have such promise that a smart investor would write checks for millions to someone who possesses them, not even knowing a lot about the nature of the business itself. That can be you and your team.

So, now let us get to the six aspects of character integrity that will help you build trust, see reality, get results, resolve problems, create growth, and find transcendent meaning.

# II

# CHARACTER DIMENSION ONE

## Establishing Trust

# building trust
# through connection

I had been called into a merger situation in the health-care industry. Two companies were becoming one, and therefore, the board
had to choose a new leader for the merged entity. One of the companies was being led by an innovator who was strong in marketing
and branding. His strengths were in casting vision, and finding how
to position a product line or service in a way that could make the
world think the fried egg had been invented for the first time. He
had experienced growth pretty much everywhere he had been.
Many thought that he would be the choice to lead the new company.

The other company was led by different guy with an entirely
different background. He was strong in operations and quantita-
tive analysis and had found ways to make complicated businesses
profitable. Known for his optimism and problem-solving abilities,

he exuded positive energy, and when he looked at any kind of obstacle, he just put his head down and fixed it. To him, no problem seemed unconquerable, and he had the temerity to tackle tough situations.

At the time, the medical industry was undergoing massive changes as managed care and HMOs were ramping up their takeover of the entire landscape. For companies to make money in the land of bundled payments, absence of third-party insurance, reimbursements of half of what had been paid for services just a few years previously, and complicated contractual panels that confused everyone as to who the customer was, was to say the least confusing and daunting. Especially when companies had built entire strategies, infrastructures, services, products, and teams to address a world that was quickly becoming nonexistent. As a result, the board chose the analytical genius, feeling that they really needed his brainpower to find a way through those complicated waters.

And, he was a nice guy.

On this particular morning, the new president was to address the upper-management teams of both companies, in their first meeting together as a team. It was that exciting day of the new blended family, where the new leader would call them to be one, cast the vision and set the tone for the new entity, and bring everyone together to become the army that would rule the world. You could feel the anticipation in the room of what a big moment this was.

The new president's strengths showed through as he gave his analysis of the industry, the forces that had driven things to where they were then, and the opportunities that had been created by such a changing world. His view was that the resources and talents of the new combined company were exactly what was needed to make all of those gloomy numbers add up to good ones. His brain clearly operated on a different plane from most, and if you were there, you no longer felt the gloom and doom of health care, but re-alized that there were still formulas by which a business could oper-ate and do well.

Then it happened. He ended his presentation and opened the room up to questions. The first was from a woman, who said, "In light of some of the strategic initiatives that you have talked about, I start to wonder what is going to happen to our division and my people. In the last few years we have done a major restructure and I have moved people from all over the country, brought some on from other companies, and put together a sizable budget to keep that going and all of them going for the next two years, at least. As I read between the lines here, with both companies somewhat in this direction, I start to wonder what is going to happen to some of the paths that we have been going down, and what might happen to some of the people. I mean, I see the possibility of some huge shake-ups with this."

You could hear the concern in her voice and even see it in her eyes when she talked about the people. She was that kind of sea-soned manager who is also coach, den mother, and career steward for people. You could tell that the people part of what she was ask-ing was as big a factor as the business question. At the same time, you got the feeling that many other managers in the room had other employees' pictures in their own heads, wondering who they might have to lay off or move. It brought a kind of immediacy to the air.

"Well, that's not going to be a problem," the new president said. "You won't have to worry about that at all because of the offshoot lines that are going to come with the merged strategy." He then gave some figures that supported his thoughts. "There is going to be plenty for them to do, and I don't think in that sector we should lose anyone. Don't worry about it. That's not going to happen. There, over there against the wall . . . what is your question?"

While the eyes of most of the room went over to the next person asking a question, I was fixated on the woman who'd asked the first one. It was as if her eyes glazed over. *He had totally missed her.* It did not matter one iota what he had said about the numbers, or whether there were going to be a zillion new product lines. It did not even matter if he was right. What mattered, as the eyes told, was that he had not come close to understanding what it was like to be in her shoes, leading hundreds of people who had moved families, given up other jobs, and trusted her with their futures. He did not get it that she had to face tons of e-mails and phone calls from real people who were scared, and she was scared for them. And he also did not get that his quick answer was not going to fix that. And, *she got it that he didn't get it,* as did others in the room.

*[handwritten margin note: Didn't make a connection]*

The next question came from a man about the strategy itself: "When you said that we can merge some of our existing lines into the managed-care sales force, I wonder how that is going to work. My experience is that the teams that call on doctors have very different backgrounds and strengths than the ones who hammer out the contracts with payers. I am concerned about how we merge those two cultures and get them on the same page. I can see some of the salespeople bottoming out in the big institutional environments. It could be really rocky." As he said that, others in the room were nodding, leaning over and whispering to each other the way people do when someone has hit upon something they feel.

"That won't get in the way," the new president quickly said. "The new product lines themselves will take care of whatever their backgrounds lack. They will virtually sell themselves, so the people will adapt very quickly and actually be a lot better off. The numbers just are on their side."

I looked at that the man with the question. He had a little bit of a steel-eyed stare with a quizzical note. I could tell it was not the expression of "What am I missing here?" but more "Is he seriously thinking there are going to be no problems with our salespeople?"

It was as if he could not quite believe that this concern had so quickly been dismissed and explained away. The room was a little quieter than it had been a moment ago.

"Who's next?" the president asked.

"I have a question," another man said. "What is going to happen to our benefits package? There are a lot of differences in the two companies and the ways things are covered, and vested. I know that a big part of our group's motivation comes from some of the security stuff we have built in, and is that going to be enlarged to cover the other side of the company, or are we going to shift to theirs? It will mean that we have to redo a lot of compensation packages, I think."

"That will work out OK. I think when people get the big picture of what is happening here, they will be happy with the overall net. Whatever their benefits package said before is going to be overshadowed by the new possibilities. They will love it," the president encouraged. What he did not see was that people were *not* going to love trying to walk their teams through to the place where they loved it. The questioner knew that in between changing an employee's benefits and that person's "loving the future" was the employee's twelve-year-old's asthma machine and many emergency-room visits.

You could feel the air kind of going out of the room. People were still attentive and focused on the president, but the feeling had changed. It was nothing bad or any big elephant in the room. But, the energy was gone. I could see people's faces and their eyes glazing over. They were just no longer there. I know from experience when an audience is with you and when they aren't, and this group had exited.

The president fielded some more of their questions and talked about another initiative or two, then ended the meeting. He and I walked out of the room and through some double doors into a lobby. Before the doors had completely swung shut, he turned to me with an exuberant smile on his face and said, "Wasn't that *great!* It went so well." You could feel his energy.

"No!" I said. "No! It wasn't great at all. It was one of the worst meetings I have ever sat through. You completely lost them. You did not connect with one of their concerns whatsoever. You just systematically went through the room and told them why what they were concerned about wasn't true. You invalidated all of their experiences and fears.

"I am telling you, you missed them big-time and you are going to have to do something to get them back. It was awful." I surprised myself a little at how strongly I came out of the gate with him, but it was so true.

"That's not true," he said, a puzzled look on his face. "I didn't do that!"

"See? You just did it again, right then, to *me*. You just negated and invalidated what I was trying to tell you. You didn't hear it at all. You're not getting it when people tell you what they are experiencing. That is what I mean, right there." I went on to try to explain to him how he did that, and he just didn't get it.

Why? Not because of a lack of talent, brains, or competencies. It was because of the lack of character integrity in the manner we have described: "unified, whole, undivided, unimpaired, and sound in construction." As I followed him through the next year, I could see the lack of those things in this situation, in his entire wake.

*In less than a year, he was gone.*

Now, here is the point. He was a *very* nice guy, a caring guy. He would have thrown himself in front of the train for any of those people and also for their employees and their families that he had never met. That is just the kind of person he was. When a receptionist in his office was having a birthday, or some other occasion, he was the one who would get everyone to buy a gift, get a cake, and

*[handwritten marginal note: He didn't truly care for people]*

hang up the balloons. He loved to make people feel good and treated them well.

But, and this is a big but, his makeup was *impaired and not whole*. Although he was a caring person, he was unable to connect with what people were really thinking, feeling, and experiencing. As a result, as much as he cared, they often did not experience that he really understood and often felt that he just missed them altogether. He could be nice and cheer everyone up, but he did not tune in to what people were experiencing, feeling, thinking, in a way that made them feel that he had heard their hearts. ← *connect in these ways*

That is what happened in that meeting and continued to happen in his leadership. He could not make people feel as if he entered into their reality, so although he had their attention through his position, *he did not have their hearts.* And this was not only with regard to the emotional material such as the woman who was concerned about her people, but also with the real business and strategic realities that other people had as well. He would hear the facts, but if he had another reality, they would not know that he had heard them at all.

To illustrate, let's go back to that meeting and see what he was missing. When the woman talked about the people she had moved and the things that they had poured themselves into for two years, what if his makeup was one that actually *drove* him to enter into her experience? What if he possessed the kind of empathy that *desired* to know what it was like for her and what she was going through? In short, to be there with her, instead of telling her why her experience was wrong. It would have sounded something like this instead:

*"Wow, you've poured a lot of yours and other people's lives into this. How long have you guys been going down this path?"*

*"Really . . . how many people have you moved? That must have been really hard to make that call, and also for them to do it. How did it go? Was the restructure messy?"*

*"I can see if I am in your shoes why you would be worried for them. They have*

*got to be scared too. . . . What have they been saying to you? I mean, they have had all of this change and now another one. . . . Anyone close to leaving?"*

*"So you're dealing with some people who must be really on pins and needles. I'm glad you're worried about them."*

*"Of course I can understand your concern. I would be feeling like that too. Let me tell you what my thoughts are on it, and then you tell me what that sounds like. Tell me if you think it will help them or if we need to understand more."*

Can you feel the difference in the room? If he were leaning into her reality and experience, and joining it, they would have been together, and the room would have been right there with them too. He would have had them because they would have felt as if he really understood and connected with where they were and what they were experiencing. And by "having them," I don't mean in a manipulative way. He would have them in a real way because he really cared and was putting his arms around their experience. They would have each other.

Now, here is an important point. Perhaps, in the end, *he would have made no different decisions from the ones he had made.* Perhaps he was exactly right about the new opportunities blowing away anything that they were previously doing, and it would truly be good in the end, just as he said. If he had understood their concerns, he would not have had to change anything in the end. He was the leader, and it was going to be his call ultimately. Understanding someone doesn't mean that you will necessarily agree with them. main point!!!

But it does mean that if you are going to get them to come *with* you in your final decision, and trust you, you have to understand where they are and join them in that place first. If you have kids in Phoenix that you want to take to Disney World, no matter how good it is going to be for them, they have to want to get in the car. And people are not going to get in the car with someone they don't trust or don't feel understands them. We trust people who we think hear us, understand us, and are able to empathize with our realities as well as their own. That is why the abilities to connect and trust are so intertwined.

## More Than Caring: Being Nice Is Not Enough

In the end trust is about the heart, and someone making an investment in you from his or her heart. And if you gain people's trust, their heart, then you also have their desire and passion. Heart, desire, and passion all go together. Without one, you don't have the other. That is why some leaders only get *compliance,* but can't capture their people's best efforts. It is why some parents get obedience in the short term, but not autonomous kids who *desire* to be the best for them that they can be. These leaders and parents just impose their will on the other people.

But the good ones capture the other people's will, their true desire, through connecting with them first. It is the difference in the parent who tells the teenager to "get with it and stop hanging out with 'those kids,' " and the one who sits down and tries to find out what the teen is *getting* from hanging out with "those kids." What part of the child's heart are those kids able to capture that the parent and the parent's values have not? That is the only way that a parent can move a child past compliance to being "willing" to come the parent's way.

*Will* is an interesting term. We usually think of it in terms of volition and choice. "Will you do something?" is asking if you would choose to do a particular thing. But, in another sense, for example in Greek, *will* means to "desire" or "delight" in something. If you "will it," then it is what you truly *want.* Anyone who has ever tried to depend on "willpower," for example, to stop doing something he or she truly desired has seen which one wins out in the end. "Willpower" and just trying to make good choices cannot compete with the true *desire* of the heart, for that is where the passion is. You will not lose weight, for example, until your deepest desire is to get healthy. The heart is always stronger than mere "willpower."

So, how far do you think the people in that room were going to go down the hard road of change for someone who did not connect with their hearts? How much *desire* did they now have to sacrifice for the mission? Not very far, and not very much. They might be "committed" to their duty, but they were not committed to following him.

How far will a spouse go for someone who makes no attempt to understand and connect with where he or she is and what he or she is experiencing in the relationship? As time goes on, less and less. The love begins to wane, and the passion fails to fuel the commitment as it once did. That is when they get into danger if they do not have a deeper desire to live out their values and commitments, over and above how they feel, as we shall see later. But, if someone feels understood, and connected with, it is a whole different story.

We can see this not only in the big examples, such as a corporate merger, saving a teenager from the wrong crowd, or making a marriage work, but even in the smallest ones as well. You have probably had the experience I had the other day in a restaurant. I ordered some soup and it was barely room temperature. I love soup. But, I hate it cold.

I called the server over and said, "Excuse me, but my soup is cold."

Immediately, he said, "That's horrible. You didn't come all this way to have cold soup. That's the worst. Here, let me get you some more."

I loved it. He understood. I remember thinking, "I'll be back." I had not even eaten the soup yet, but I felt as if someone was on my team.

Sometimes there is nothing that can be done. But, to know

someone understands makes it somehow different. "You know, you're right. It is cold, and I wouldn't want it that way either. But, our ___ just broke and I can't heat it. It's pretty bad, huh? What else can I get you?"

I might be disappointed at the soup, but I like the restaurant. They are interested in what it is like for me. But what if the server says, "It looks fine to me, It should be OK. I tasted it a little while ago. But, if you don't want it, I'll get you something else." There is a disconnect here and it is not the same. I don't sense his heart. Who gets the bigger tip?

The second waiter might even be "nice," as was our ousted leader. But, he didn't understand. The one who understands is the one who wins a customer who will not only choose to come back, but actually wants to.

This is about more than being "nice." All leadership or success literature will tell you that you have to be nice and not a jerk. People actually do research on topics like that too. They have proven that mean, antagonistic, and adversarial leaders or bosses do not build thriving cultures or people. Imagine that. Who funded that research?

*The bigger questions have more to do with why the seemingly "good guys" don't do well.* Why do the "nice couples" get divorced? Why do the "loving parents" have kids that go sideways and join countercultures? Why can't some really nice leaders capture the hearts of their people? It is sometimes because when it comes to human behavior, being nice is not enough. We have to be connected with, and that is a whole different dimension of character. What is that dimension?

## Involvement in the "Other"

Fundamentally, what undergirds this component of character is *involvement in the "other."* Connection is the opposite of "detachment," whereby a person is a kind of island unto him- or herself. Now, don't confuse that with being introverted, or extroverted. Those are styles that can be used in the service of either connectedness or detachment. You can be very extroverted, and even nice to people, and never establish a deep bond. In fact, an extrovert's wordiness can even serve to keep people at bay and never allow them in.

Detachment is about not crossing the space to actually enter into another person's world through the curiosity and desire to know them, to understand them, to be "with" them, to be present with them, and ultimately to care for them. Sadly, a lot of loving and nice people are detached in this way, and their relationships suffer for it.

People feel cared about, and trust is built, when they know that we have a genuine interest in knowing them, knowing about them, and having what we know matter. I was talking to the president of a company about this concept recently, and he told me a story that he was personally affected by. He had recently had to do some layoffs in the company as a result of his parent company's directives, and it was going to be painful for some people. As they discussed it in the management team and made plans, the division leaders were assigned to take care of most of it. But, feeling for the people losing their jobs, he wanted to talk to the ones at a certain level himself. For him, it was an act of caring to do that personally. He was concerned for their pain and distress.

In one of his meetings, he told one man that he was losing his job and how sorry he was. He told him that he felt for him and understood how difficult this must be, and how he just personally wanted him to know that it was not taken lightly, and that he hoped it would all work out OK for him. He wanted him to know how valued he was. What the man said surprised him, but got his attention:

"You know, I really understand. That is business. Layoffs happen, and sometimes there is nothing that can be done about it. It is just the best business decision, and I don't in any way take it personally. It will be hard, but that is just part of the way that business works. But let me tell you what I do take personally, and what does hurt, and what does bother me.

"I work right down the hall and have been there for some time. I see you all the time. And this is the first time that you have ever said more than just a nod or 'hi' to me. You basically don't even acknowledge that I am there. That bothers me a lot more than the fact that you are laying me off."

The president was stunned. It had never occurred to him that he had done that, and I could tell he was affected by it, and he told me he would never allow that to happen again. In the midst of all the noise and work, he had allowed himself to become detached and not involved in the "other" at least to a degree that made him feel as if he mattered.

Fundamentally, connection is the experience by one person that another is invested in him or her. It begins in infancy, when a baby comes to life as its mother involves herself in its being and existence. What he or she feels and experiences matters, and a bond is built. That continues throughout childhood, and kids who grow up with deep connections are the ones who grow up secure, and most able to deal with life. We have more research that proves that than just about anything. It is a fact. What we forget, though, is that connectedness is important not just for babies and children, but all the way through life.

In work, in marriage, in parenting, in friendship, in business, connection happens when one person has a true emotional investment in the other, and the other person experiences that and it is returned. To do that requires the character that gets out of oneself long enough to know, experience, and value the "other." And, as we will see, it has to be done in a way that the "other" can experience it.

## What Builds Connection?

If nice is not enough, and heartfelt connection is what matters, how is that established? What does that kind of character actually do that wins the hearts of other people and creates successful work and personal scenarios? Let's look at some of the building blocks to connectedness.

## Empathy

If we look at our leader who didn't make it, what was he lacking? In a word, *empathy*. Empathy is the ability to enter into another person's experience and connect with it in such a way that you actually *experience* to some degree what the other person is experiencing. It is "as if" you are that other person, at least for a moment. *Empathy* comes from the Greek words meaning "in" and "feeling." It is as if you are "in the feeling" of the other.

That is what the new CEO lacked. He did not help the people see that he could be in their feeling, in their situation, in their shoes. And if we don't feel that someone knows what it is like to be us, what they say has little credibility. If he could have entered into their feeling, and if he could have had them understand that he understood, his answers, which were probably right, would have been embraced. As it turns out, the things he said were in fact more right than not, but he was not around long enough even to get to say, "I told you so." That's another thing truly empathic people would never say anyway. Being right is not their highest value. Understanding and connecting with others is.

Empathy requires a few character components. First, there is the ability to feel and be what is referred to as softhearted. If people are cut off from their emotions to begin with, then they usually have little ability to feel what someone else is feeling. To be an empathic person means that you have overcome character *detachment*. It means that first of all, you are not detached from your own emotions. This does not mean sentimental, which in and of itself is usually false, pseudo-emotion. It means that you are truly in touch with your real feeling capacities. People who are out of touch with their own feelings are limited in their ability to empathize with others.

Second, it means that you have good boundaries. That means that when you feel what someone else is feeling, you also realize that it is *their* experience and not yours. Boundaries are the component of character whereby we realize our separateness from another person. People who lose themselves in what another person is feeling are usually not helpful. They overidentify and then do goofy things. The parent who overidentifies with his or her child's experience loses the ability to be either a support *or* a disciplinarian. It truly is a "this is going to hurt me more than it is going to hurt you" scenario, and they are not helpful when they get to that place. They can't walk through things with the child and remain separate.

In reality, it is not the parent's loss or fear or behavior problem. Parents have to realize that, and that they can't live the child's life or make the pain not exist. But, conversely, if their boundaries are too strong and they can't reach over the wall and empathize, then the connection is lost. It is a balance. When you empathize, you feel for the other person, but still know it is not *your* experience. In that way, you can be a bridge to a new and different experience from the one they are having, such as hope.

Third, and somewhat the sine qua non of empathy, is the ability to listen in a way that *communicates understanding*. When we listen, we hear. And it may be that we understand. *But, if we cannot communicate our listening in a way that lets the other person know we have truly understood, empathy has not occurred.* There is no connection.

Chances are that the CEO was listening, and that he heard. If you gave him a test on each questioner's content, he could probably give you the data. He could say that the first one was concerned about her people and the upset of an entire direction that they had been moving, and the second was concerned about the disconnect between two types of sales forces and their potential customers, and the third about people's needs for benefits and security. But, just because he heard it and got the data did not mean that he had listened in a way that communicates understanding. Empathy had not occurred.

True listening and understanding occurs only when

> the other person understands
> that you understand.

And that only happens when your character is connecting enough to get out of your own experience and into the experience of the other. To do that requires a makeup that is not detached, or self-focused. It is to truly cross the divide, or as Martin Buber called it, to establish the "I-Thou" relationship. The other person is a person, and not an "it," or an object. He or she is a real human to you that you experience and connect with, and he knows that because your connection drives you to express it:

"This merger sounds like it has thrust some real heavy issues into all of your lives, and today I want to make sure that I understand what's going on and how we can walk through that together."

Can you imagine the energy that would have been in that room had he begun the Q and A that way? He would have had the beginning of a real team that worked together to become one, as each shared what his or her experience was and how things were being affected. People would have piped in to help each other as the empathy for each other grew. I have seen this dynamic and it is awesome. You begin to hear things like "Well, I found a great relocation coach for my direct reports. Let's bring your team into those groups and you can join us." Or, "That's gross. I have been through that in my former job. Here is what I did, and it helped clear everything up." Unity forms around mutual care based in empathy. But it comes from getting out of your own experience and into the experience of what it is like to be the other person, and then completing the loop by letting them know that you have heard it. It happens like this:

They talk → you experience them → you share what you have heard and experienced about their experience → then they experience you as having heard them. They then know you are "with them."

When it is communicated to them like that, then not only did you hear and understand, but *the other person understands that you understand,* and the connection has occurred. It does not occur, and the other person's heart has not joined you, until that loop has happened. That takes an open and caring heart on your part.

Recently I spoke about this issue at a leadership conference with presidents of companies. That evening, a man walked up to me at a party and told me the following story:

"I own a manufacturing company in the Pacific Northwest and for the last year have been working on an acquisition. There is another company that would do great things for us strategically, and I have been going full bore to try to move the deal along. But, my COO and my CFO are really against it. They have been saying that for a while.

"All along, I have thought that they were just dragging the deal down and I was bugged at their attitudes. The environment around there has not been good, and things have broken down and are just kind of negative. I could feel the divide between us even when we were working on other things.

"But today, after the session on this 'connecting thing' [even business guys get it], I went back to my room and called the COO. I told him that when I got back from this trip, I wanted just the two of us to go off for a day so I could just listen to his concerns about the merger. I told him that I figured out that I have really not been listening and haven't really understood what the issues were that he was so concerned about, and that *I really wanted to get it now.*

"When I said that, there was a silence on the other end of the phone, and then he said, *'You would do that? Really?'* You could hear the shock in his voice. And then he just started talking a mile a minute. *You could feel the energy come back into our relationship.* He was his old self again, and I could remember what I liked and valued about him so much. I could tell that, no matter what happened, things were going to be a lot different. It was just such a different connection.

"So I just wanted you to encourage people to do that more. It is huge and I am going to look forward to just going back and seeing what these guys have been thinking and feeling about this thing. Who knows, I might really have missed something, but either way, it is going to be good."

It was such a cool thing to see someone moving out of his own experience and connecting with the ones he was trying to lead instead of just pulling them along, imposing his will. The energy that he felt is the natural by-product of connectedness. It is the *life force* that fuels all sorts of drive, passion, and accomplishment, in every aspect of life. And, it was the opposite of the absence of energy that was in the room in the example above with the CEO of the healthcare company. In that situation, as well as this guy's small company before the phone call, the atmosphere was more of a dull, lifeless depression. Sometimes it is vague and hard to explain, but it is never hard to feel for someone who is aware. Just check your memory and you will remember a time where you walked out of a meeting with a boss or someone else and turned to a friend and said, "He didn't get it." You know what not being heard is like, and that is why the connected character never wants to produce that experience in anyone he cares about. He never wants anyone to feel that "he didn't get it."

## The Connection and Trust Killer

If entering into another person's reality, validating it, and treating it with respect builds connection, what destroys it? The exact opposite: *invalidation.* Invalidation occurs when a person's experience is all that exists to him or her. And he or she then moves to negate the other person's experience, treating it as somehow not real or nonexistent. This is what our CEO did above. He immediately gave his reality with no space for the other people's reality to exist:

"Well, that's not going to be a problem."

"You won't have to worry about that."

"That won't get in the way."

"They will love it."

Those statements, even though they really reflect how *he* felt, are so far from where the others were at that moment that it was like trying to shake hands across the Grand Canyon. While these things might even be true, when he says them immediately without connecting with the other person first, they annihilate the other person's reality and shut him or her down. It was the same thing that he did to me in the lobby as we stepped out. My experience was that the meeting was awful. When I said that, he just quickly did away with everything that I thought or felt about it. "That's not true," he said, without connecting with what my experience was at all. He just negated it.

The sticky wicket for people who don't connect occurs when they really do have a different reality from the other person, and sometimes even a set of facts that they know are true. At those times, it feels crazy for them to "join" into someone else's "truth" that they know is just wrong or incorrect. They are afraid to validate if they disagree, because they fear it sounds as if they are giving credibility to something they know is not right.

But that is not the issue. Of course, communication is often about persuasion and bringing one person around to a different perspective. To empathize and validate what someone is experiencing does not mean that you always agree or even think that the other person is right. It just means that you see it as *valid in that it is really their experience,* and true for that person, and you show them that you understand what they are thinking and feeling. And that comes from seeing and caring about another person's heart, and communicating that, whether or not you agree. You must connect first.

But other times it means that if you did connect with it, you would learn from the other person as well and may even change what you feel about it. That is how communicating helps us to know the other person and thereby enlarge our understanding about reality. I remember a consulting project one time where there was a breakdown between two departments of a construction company. They had an ongoing conflict because the people in the field were not getting cost reports to the accounting department on schedule, and the accounting people were perpetually upset with them. In return, the field people were tired of being seen as a problem and were going sour on the relationship with the home office.

When I got them together, each was telling me their side of things and why the other ones were wrong and not being reasonable. They were only interested in the other people seeing why their view was right. The accounting people were talking about schedules and when they wanted the reports and such, and the field guys were talking about the work that had to get done that was more important than paperwork. They were getting nowhere fast. At that point I saw an opening.

I asked one of the women who worked in accounting to talk

about what her day is like when the field people do not get the numbers to her. She said that first she puts in a reminder call. When she does that, the assistant on the other end has to go check on it. While she is waiting, her boss comes in and gets frustrated with the delay. He puts pressure on her. She feels tense.

Then, she begins to get behind on other things. Other calls come regarding things she was supposed to do while she was tracking down the delay. Then she is further behind from putting out those fires. You could see the domino effect happening until she got to the end of the day and said, "Then, by the time I finally get them, I have to stay late to get them typed up for the next day when they are needed for the review meeting with the project managers, and . . ." Her voice broke and her eyes filled with tears. "Sorry," she said. "But when I get home late, I miss time with my daughter."

When I say that I saw an opening, I did not foresee this. I wanted the field people to hear the reality of the accounting people's work lives and how their own behavior affected their day, and then I thought empathy would kick in when they saw the difficulties that they were creating for them. Little did I know that the chain of effects would continue all the way to a three-year-old's life. Once they got to *that* awareness, empathy led to desire, and that led to change. But, as long as invalidation of the other side was occurring, that never happened.

The accounting people had to stop invalidating the field people as well and hear what it was like for them to have to stop and meet numbers schedules in a way that interrupted their project work. When that was finally heard, the two sides came together and found a solution in having a floating window of time that worked better for both. And they were happy. Finally.

Connection and trust happen when one heart meets another. Invalidation wipes out the other heart and closes it off. Think of the contexts of life that change when a person has the ability to connect with the other: In business, deals are won and sales are made. Employees and employers serve each other better and disputes go away. Conflicts are resolved within contractual relationships and lawsuits are avoided. Medical malpractice lawsuits are avoided when a doctor listens and understands what the patient or family has experienced as a result of an error. In personal relationships, marriages are healed when a closed-off spouse finally hears and understands what the other has been feeling and experiencing. Wayward children are won back when they feel that their side of things is finally listened to, and vice versa. Extended-family and adult-children situations are restored when each begins to connect with the other. There is not a context of life where listening and connecting with the other side's reality and experience is not helpful.

The sad thing is that most times the people who invalidate other people's experience are not aware that they are doing something destructive. In fact, they often think they are helping. The CEO, as revealed by his comment to me, thought he had been helpful to people in the meeting. When he says, "Oh, that won't be a problem," he thinks he has alleviated someone's anxiety. In reality, he has heightened it.

We have all seen those instances where someone (maybe even ourselves) has said something negative like "I'm such a loser," and someone immediately comes back with "Don't say that! You don't really feel that way!" or some other attempt to help that only drives the person further into hopelessness. The reason is that he now has two problems instead of one. He has the initial problem that he felt so negative about, and then he feels that he is all alone and has no one who truly understands. That is why people who try to help others by talking them out of what they feel are usually no help at all. It is also the reason why research has for decades proven that you can help desperate people immensely by giving them no answers at all, and only giving them empathy.

Further, other research has shown that emotional invalidation is the basis of many character disorders that lead people to psychiatric illnesses as well as poor performance in academics. It has been shown to be a factor in almost all that is wrong with people, physiological and organic causes notwithstanding. "Stop crying or I'll give you something to cry about!" does more than make a child be quiet. It disengages the child from her own feelings and inner states. As a result, she can develop a host of impulse problems as well as emotional and relational issues that affect her functioning.

The real reason for that breakdown lies in the breakdown in the structure relationship itself, which is where we get all of our capacities for performance. As the child disengages from the parent or caretaker, he or she has lost connection with the source of the functions that he needs to learn and internalize. So, impulse control, discipline, empathy, reality testing, emotional regulation, hope, trust, judgment, and the other things that children get from caretakers have all become unavailable as the connection is lost. The child is now alone, and without the capacities he or she needs.

Fast-forward to leadership, or marriage. *If the leader, in our case the CEO, had not given the "stop crying, there is nothing wrong" message, the connection would have been established to give to his people all of the things needed to meet the goals.* The discipline, hope, judgment, and creativity could have flourished. But, in his failure, the room went void. In marriage, the same thing happens. The spouses who connect find ways in the connection to control their destructive impulses, get to a higher sense of functioning in their conflict, and transcend whatever issue was driving it. By restoring the connection through empathy, they are elevated to a higher level of functioning. From childhood to corporate boardrooms, connection is key, and invalidation is a cancer. Work environments designed to solve problems are actually structured up and transformed to higher levels of functioning through empathy.

## The Costs of Not Having a Connecting Character

"I don't understand it," Sheila said. "We built this business together from the ground up, and then she goes and betrays me like this. I just cannot imagine why she would do that."

What Sheila didn't know was that I did. I totally understood it, because Sarah, her partner, had called me about a month before and asked for my help. She told me that she had some "concerns" about the way that Sheila was running things and hinted at some ethical issues. She did not exactly come out and say it, but I could tell that she was trying to cast aspersions on Sheila's character.

The conversation made me uncomfortable. People who call someone to get help for someone they are concerned about do not sound the way that she did. It seemed to me that she was trying to enlist me as an ally. I passed.

But, I did understand it. What had happened was what businesses, families, churches, departments, and organizations see every day, a classic split. There is a person who is dissatisfied in some way, similar to the one above who did not like the acquisition his boss was planning. Typically, that person has been trying to "get the ear" of a leader, partner, or colleague about some problem, or perceived problem, for a while. But the other person invalidates his or her experience, thinking that he or she is negative or a whiner or just doesn't get it and should get over it. In whatever way it happens, the other person just does not hear and connect with the person's complaints. After a while, the complaining person becomes discouraged about not being heard and unplugs. Feeling hopeless, the person *disconnects from the other person and gives up.*

But, although people have given up on being heard by the other, they have not given up on being heard by someone. Anyone, almost. But, usually, they look for someone who is in a position to join them in some way against the first person, as opposed to someone who will help resolve the conflict. They are looking for allies against the other person that they feel hurt and discounted by. And, they can usually find some, either at the coffee machine or in the boardroom.

In an organization, it is not uncommon for a person to find another key employee or two, or several, with whom he can share his experience. Discovering a sympathetic ear, he talks about how the other person is unethical, uncaring, self-centered, domineering, incompetent, or in some other way impugns the person's character and personhood. In marriage, the spouse who feels invalidated and not connected with will find that listening ear in someone of the opposite sex. The roots of an affair begin at the sympathetic ear. In families, one of the members has a gripe against someone else in the extended family and splits the group against the "problem" person.

This is exactly what had happened in Sheila's scenario. Sarah had felt invalidated for a long time and was discounted by Sheila. So, she found some support. First in some key employees, and then with a couple of investors who had themselves felt discounted by Sheila. As a result, they came together and split the company. Sheila was ousted, and Sarah was launched in a new venture, taking half of the employees with her.

"How could this have happened?" was Sheila's overwhelming feeling. "We were best friends and partners. I can't believe that she would do this to me. I just can't believe it."

I had to try to explain to her that she had helped it to happen by discounting and invalidating Sarah's experience for several years. Sarah had tried to talk; Sheila did not listen. Finally, Sarah had gone somewhere else. And this is the danger that nonconnectors do not get:

> The human heart will seek to be known,
> understood, and connected with above all else.
> If you do not connect, the ones you care about
> will find someone who will.

So, people find themselves flabbergasted to learn:

- That their spouse has found someone new.
- That half of the employees are going to join the number two person in the new start-up.
- That half of the family has "turned against me."
- That half of their church is going to leave and go down the street and start a new one.

And many times it could have been prevented if the person knew how to connect. Now, that in no way justifies what the other people have done. Obviously people of mature character would not have created a split like that. They would have tried to help resolve the conflict and be a helpful and not a divisive force. That is what a good intervention does, for example. Its intent is not to divide, but to unify around the problem person and get him or her to finally get it. Everyone is on her side and pulling for her in that scenario. In the above ones, the other people did not do that, so they obviously have their own issues and created more problems than they solved, such as an unnecessary split.

Again, the point always is that *character meets the demands of reality*. Someone who is adept at connecting would have seen the disconnect occurring and would have taken proactive steps to repair it and make unity happen instead. Then, if the other person did not cooperate, he or she would have been exposed as a problem person without support. But in these scenarios, because people are not listened to, they often emerge as the poor "victim" of the nonconnecting leader, and others are glad to rescue them from such a terrible person.

If Sheila had been a connecting listener, able to enter the reality of another person, she would have heard Sarah's discontent as valid. Maybe not right or justified, but valid. It was true for her. And then Sheila would have treated it with the respect that it deserved. That might have been to try to help Sarah to come to a better understanding of reality, if Sarah was truly in la-la land. In that process of really hearing and getting to the bottom of it, it would have become clear over time if Sarah had her own agenda and was twisting reality. She would then have gotten no support, because Sheila's efforts to hear and understand would have revealed Sarah's issues. Sarah would not have been seen as a victim, but a divider.

Or, if Sarah was really listened to and joined with, Sheila might have found that Sarah was right. Sheila might have found that she needed to change some things, and then resolution would have occurred. The point is that, either way, Sheila played a part in the demise of the situation by being detached and clueless about what was going on. Had she listened, she would not have lost her company.

## Connecting Character That Meets the Demands of Reality

For the most part, life involves people. That is obvious in the sphere of relationships, such as friendship, family, marriage, and community. But, we are often unaware of how big the people part is in getting work done as well. It is just as vital. So, if your character is going to meet the demands of reality, it is going to have to be able to negotiate the world of people. And that can only be done successfully through connectedness.

To some, it seems like psychobabble, as if it has little to do with business or success. But, it really does. What if, for example, you led a company with almost $50 billion in revenues, and you found out that over half of your employees were ready to leave and go to another company if they had a chance? Would you think that you had a business problem? I would hope so. That kind of data would get the attention of any good CEO. What a precarious spot to be in.

What kind of business problem would cause that? Poor strategy? Poor benefits? Poor compensation? Sometimes. But what if I said that it had something to do with emotional detachment, nonconnectedness, and a lack of listening by the leadership? That sounds like something out of a marriage retreat, not a business journal.

But that is exactly what *Business Week* magazine reported in its November 3, 2003, issue regarding Dell Computers:

> When Dell CEO Michael S. Dell and President Kevin B. Rollins met privately in the fall of 2001, they felt confident that the company was recovering from the global crash in PC sales. Their own personal performance, however, was another matter. Internal interviews revealed that subordinates thought Dell, 38, was impersonal and emotionally detached, while Rollins, 50, was seen as autocratic and antagonistic. Few felt strong loyalty to the company's leaders. Worse, the discontent was spreading: a survey taken over the summer, following the company's first-ever mass layoffs, found that half of Dell Inc.'s employees would leave if they got the chance.
>
> What happened next says much about why Dell is the best-managed company in technology. At other industry giants, the CEO and his chief sidekick might have shrugged off the criticism or let the issue slide. Not at Dell. Fearing an exodus of talent, the two execs focused on the gripes. Within a week, Dell faced his top 20 managers and offered a frank self-critique, acknowledging that he is hugely shy and that it sometimes makes him seem aloof and unapproachable. He vowed to forge tighter bonds with his team. Some in the room were shocked. They knew personality tests given to key execs had repeatedly shown Dell to be an "off-the-charts introvert," and such an admission from him had to have been painful. "It was powerful

*stuff," says Brian Wook, the head of the public-sector sales for the Americas. "You could tell it wasn't easy for him."*

*Michael Dell didn't stop there. Days later, they began showing a video-tape of his talk to every manager in the company—several thousand people. Then Dell and Rollins adopted desk props to help them do what didn't come naturally. A plastic bulldozer cautioned Dell not to ram through ideas without including others, and a Curious George encouraged Rollins to listen to his team before making up his mind.*

Listen to some of the actual words there: *impersonal, emotionally detached, autocratic, antagonistic, loyalty, focused on the gripes, shy, aloof, unapproachable, tighter bonds, including others, listen to his team.* These are not usually the things you hear in business and success training, but they are the things of reality. No matter how huge the success that Dell's talents, brains, competencies, and alliances had brought about, there still was this thing we called the wake that has to do with a person's makeup. And as I told the boys in chapter 1, ultimately we all have to pay attention to it, because attention *will be given to it.* Attention from half of a workforce leaving a company is a lot of attention. **It is better if we do it proactively as Michael Dell did.** Don't we wish all CEOs would heed that kind of feedback and take those kinds of bold steps, or spouses, or parents? It would solve a lot of problems.

The reality to see here is that *this stuff matters.* Connecting with others in a way that makes them feel understood and valued is key to life and the basis of building trust and loyalty. From that base, everything else works. To do that requires the kind of character that is oriented toward others and makes proactive connections with them in a way that builds bonds. In the next chapter, we will take a look at another aspect of character that builds trust.

# 5

· · · · · · · · · · · · · · · · · · · · · · ·

# building trust
# through extending favor

I hate it when people are thinking of doing business with someone they know I have had dealings with, and they ask me if they should go forward, when my experience tells me that I would not want to go there again, and I have to be honest and tell them that. Now, if the person is an absolute criminal or evil or really bad in some way, I have little qualm in saying so. The hard one is when the other person is basically good, would never lie, cheat, or steal, and is competent, and someone I am on good terms with. But, something else is wrong, and it is something that the person never would recognize as being "wrong." But it is one of the key essentials that builds trust.

Let me give you an example of a call like that I got several years ago. I was asked about the person's "integrity." I gulped, as I really wanted to be able to give that clear and unadulterated "Awesome!

Go for it! You will love working with him!" kind of answer. But here is what I had to say instead:

"I am fumbling a little bit here to get this right. I really like Joe, and he is enormously talented. He is honest and will not lie, cheat, or steal. He will basically do what he tells you he will do. So all of that is good, and you can trust it."

"So, what are you stumbling over or not saying?" my friend asked.

"Well, here is the only way I know how to say it. Make sure that, in writing, you absolutely, one hundred percent protect your interests and get contracts and commitments for everything you are going to need. Make sure that everything that is important to you is protected, in writing."

"That sounds awful, like he is not trustworthy. If he is so honest and has integrity, why would I have to worry so much about watching out for my interests?" my friend asked, somewhat confused.

I understood his confusion, as it is the kind of confusion that people feel when there is a basically good person in their life that they would not, for some reason, trust with the deepest aspects of their heart. How could I explain it?

"Here is the best way to say it . . . you have to worry about your interests *because he is not going to,*" I said. "He will not lie to you or steal from you, and he will do what he says he is going to do. But, he is only going to be thinking about what is good for him, not what is good for you. He is not going to be looking out for your interests, *so make sure you do.* That is what I mean."

"I still don't quite understand," my friend said.

"I would have ironclad contracts with really smart lawyers so he will have to do what you need, and not do what you don't want. If you do that and negotiate those things up front, then you will be happy."

My friend went ahead and did the deal. It worked out well for him and was successful. About three years later, I ran into him at a party, and he walked up to me and said, "Thank you for your advice. I did exactly what you told me to do, and it has worked out well. But I one hundred percent see what you were talking about, and if I had not tied everything up very tight, I would not like where I would be now. He does what he agrees to, but is not really looking out for anybody else in the process. There are things he would not have done if I had not tied him up contractually. So, if I had not done that, I don't think it would be so good."

"Glad it worked out," I said. "Would you do it again?"

He just looked at me.

I knew what that meant.

## Trustworthy Character at the Next Level

In one sense, the person that we were discussing was "trustworthy." He could be trusted to do what was agreed to. If he said that he was going to provide something in the deal, he most likely would. You could trust what you had agreed to. Great. Great? Just make sure that you think ahead enough to cover everything you need. Because if something comes up that you did not think of or was not foreseen and does not fit his need, then chances are that it is not going to happen. In short, you still have to look out for yourself.

But, there is a much greater degree of trust in the person of a more complete integrity. It is the kind of trust that *looks out for your interests, as well as his or her own.* In other words, you are not in it alone. There is someone who is not only looking out for what is good for him, but what is good for you too. That goes past just "win-win," meaning that he will look out for you when it benefits him. It goes to looking out for you, period.

One of the Hebrew words that means "trust" has the association that I like most when thinking of what "trust" actually means:

To trust means to be *careless.*

It means that you do not have to worry about how to "take care" of yourself with that person, because he is going to be worried about that too. It means that you do not have to "guard" yourself with her, because she is going to be concerned with what is good for you and what is not good for you. You do not have to "watch your back" with him, because he is going to be watching it for you. So, if something comes up in the deal later that neither of you thought of, you know that the person on the other side of the table is going to be concerned for your interests as well as his own. He won't be a pushover and ignore what he needs, but he will have concern for you too, even when he doesn't have to.

A friend who owns a manufacturing company told me a story about a survey that they did once where they found that the employees felt that their benefits package was not as good as it should be. On first glance at the results, he was a little ticked at their being disgruntled, as they were well compensated, and past that, he knew that the company spent more on benefits than any of its competitors. He had allocated the budget for it and knew that it was true. So, his first impulse was to give them a lesson on being appreciative and content.

But, being a person of integrated character, he held back and decided to do further research as to what was behind this. He found that he was indeed spending more than any of his competitors for benefits. But, he was not getting a lot for his money, and there absolutely were better benefit packages out there. His employees were not getting the best that they could get, which was his commitment and promise to them beforehand. He commissioned HR to go find the best package out there and report back to him. And they found one, a lot better than the one the employees had, and *at a big savings to the company*. The benefits were not only better, but cheaper too.

Now, here is where his character kicks in. He could have bought the new package, announced it to the employees, and told them he had listened and they had gotten what he had promised, which was the best package in the market, and saved the company money. And I am sure they would have been thrilled. But that is not what he did.

What he did was think, "Wait, we have already budgeted this amount for the benefits. It is a line item and we can afford it and have allocated it to the people. Now, since the benefits cost less than that, let's take the savings and put it in a trust for them to enhance their retirement package. In my thinking, it is money that was set aside for them already, and now that we don't have to spend it on the other benefits, let's give them the savings."

When he announced that to the company, four things happened, and the fourth is by far the biggest.

First, the employees discovered that they could trust him to *listen* to them when they said that something was not good for them. He had taken the survey seriously and had done something about it. They were "heard" in the way that we discussed in the last chapter.

Second, they could trust him to do what he had promised, that is to get them the best benefits possible. He fulfilled his promise and could be "trusted" to do what he had said he would do. His word was true.

Third, they got a big windfall benefit that they did not expect. They were given "more" than they had thought was coming to them. They won the lottery, so to speak, and that was a good thing. An unexpected benefit.

But fourth, and this is the huge one,

They had no representation on the other side,
and their interests were still looked out for
by the other party, not by themselves.

Their interests were being looked out for when they were not looking. And that had nothing to do with "win-win," as there was no greater win for him. Now, *that is trustworthiness.* Think of how much less "on guard" they felt they had to be in any dealings they would ever have with him or the company. And that is the supreme essence of trust, not being "guarded." If all companies were run like this, *labor dispute* might be an oxymoron.

An interesting side note about this story to illustrate more of the character integration of this particular individual came from a later discussion. When I asked him more about it, he told me of another aspect of "favor" that even leads to greater trust. He said that his fear in trying to do well by people in a "unilateral" kind of way like the above example can at times feel paternalistic, or biased. It can seem like "I know what is best for you."

He says that when he tries to act on someone's best behalf that he also has to be sensitive in as many ways as possible to include them in the process, so that he is not "deciding reality for them." That was his concern in this particular incident, that he had decided to do something for them on his own. But the very fact that he would be concerned with that shows further the concept that we are talking about. He was also looking out for their interests to be a part of the process. The fear was also that their perception would be that they were not being taken care of, even though he felt that he was, another example of being concerned for the other.

Incredible things happen when two parties "let down their guard" with each other. They get open, creative, take risks, learn from each other, and deliver fruit in whatever their endeavor to a much more leveraged degree than if they were in the protected mode. This happens in personal relationships, such as marriage, friendship, or parenting, and in business as well. To get to everything that can come from two people's hearts, minds, and souls, you have to get to openness and vulnerability. You have to have *access*. And access is only given as trust increases.

When access builds, more is given. We saw in the last chapter how connecting is the first key to accessing the heart. It means that you truly know the other party. But, once you know the person, trust goes to a whole different level when you both figure out that the other is "for" you and not "against" you or even indifferent, even when you are not watching. The access gets multiplied as you want to give more of yourself to this person who truly desires the best for you.

Negotiations go very differently as defensiveness and protectiveness are not in the way. Answers and solutions are discovered as both parties work on the other's needs. As concern for those is given, transcendent things happen that could not have happened in the protective mode. Watch any couple work out a problem when they have the kind of trust that knows the other one is as concerned for them as they are for themselves, and you will see a relationship that creates a space that works for everyone. Observe a business relationship that works that way, and you will understand why their lawyers' bills are lower than other people's. It never gets "adversarial."

## "For" and Not "Against"

This kind of character has a basic stance that is "for" the other person, i.e., neither "neutral" nor "against" them. It is an orientation that gets to the deepest aspects of character, as it reflects how much someone actually values people. If they are objects, as we saw earlier, then they are to be used and manipulated, even treated well, as a means to an end. But, if they are valued as people, then they are to be treated as we treat the ones who really do matter to us, with care, concern, and intent to do good, not harm. We treat them as we would want to be treated.

You can almost divide character's ability to trust and be trustworthy into three categories, or stances. The first is what we refer to as paranoid. This kind of person just doesn't see trust as an option and can do OK, as long as things are going well. But, these people typically do not extend themselves to others in the kinds of giving and vulnerability that we saw above, because they feel as if everyone will come back to get them. Somehow they will "get screwed in the end," they feel. "No good turn goes unpunished" could be their motto, and when something goes wrong, they instantly get into retaliatory mode.

Since they can so quickly feel that you are out to get them, trusting them becomes difficult also because they will quickly turn into an adversary, based on suspicion or even a slight of some sort. And since they feel so threatened, they respond with heavy artillery and attack. You are not really safe, even when things are going well, as it could quickly turn nasty. You often hear people say of them, "You don't want to get on his or her bad side." That's because they really do perceive the world as split between the good guys and the bad guys, and because of that, they are always expecting to see the bad guy come around the corner, and that could be you. And since you can become "bad" pretty quickly, you have to watch out for them also. Everyone is on edge, and "careless trust" really never happens.

The second type of person is not really one who is suspicious or expects things to go bad. These types desire trust and good relationships and treat people well, as long as they are being treated well. And they do not turn mole hills into mountains or read paranoid meanings into innocent mistakes. They are pretty forgiving and can solve problems. They will do wonderful things as well and can be quite giving *to people who are doing well to them.* They give as long as they are receiving, and things are mutual. They truly are "for" the ones who are "for" them. In that sense, they are people who "play fair." "You treat me well, and I will treat you well" seems to be the rule that they live by.

But, if something truly does go wrong or, even less than going wrong, is not equal or mutual in some way, then they cry foul, and their good treatment of the other stops. They are not being stroked, so they are not going to stroke. "This is not a 'win-win' situation," they feel. So, what they were doing "for" the other goes away.

If you think about it, this is fair. Fair is the old "eye for an eye, and a tooth for a tooth." *Treat me well, and I will do the same. But, if you don't, then forget it.* This is also where most divorces and broken partnerships come from as well. People fall in love with each other and give to each other greatly. But, it is a *dependent* giving, and a *dependent* love. In other words, they are giving to each other because they are being given to. They are being gratified in some way, so they are giving "in return." As long as the other person gives to them, they give to the other.

When a couple fall in love and give so much to each other, they can never imagine that they might one day end in divorce. But, they do. What happens is that one becomes a little less giving, or even a little bit moody and not as loving as before. Then the other withdraws and feels unappreciated. He or she gets resentful and does not show the kind of love that he once did. Then the other feels more moody, since she is getting less, and the cycle spirals downward. Throw into the mix an outside influence that gratifies one of them, and there you have the ingredients for the affair, and then the split. But, they started off loving each other *so well. Trust seemed to be so freely given.*

The truth is that it is difficult to trust someone based on the demand for mutual performance. If I can only trust you to be for me when I am doing well by you, then I am in trouble. Because the truth is that I will fail you in some way somewhere along the path, and at that moment I need you to help me, not turn against me. But if you are going to turn on me when I fail to do my part well, then I am always in fear and protection mode, thinking that I could lose your support at any juncture. Then we live not in trust, but in mutual fear. This is what is behind most international relations, and why they are so tenuous so often. They "trust" and become "allies," but they fear also, as things could turn if one's interests are not satisfied. And the couple who live in that kind of treaty are always vulnerable to a "better deal" coming along. The love is dependent on the other one gratifying him or her.

True trust comes when we realize that another's goodness, and being for my best interest, is not dependent on anything. It is just a part of that person's integrity. It is *who that person is,* the kind of person who wants the best for others and will do whatever he or she can to bring that about. Then, there is nothing to fear. If I mess up, you will be there for me. You are going to do well by me, even if I am not watching. That doesn't mean that you are going to ignore my failures, by any measure. You may even do an intervention, or something strong to get me to face my lack of performance. But, you will still have my best interests in mind, and that will be your motivation. As a result, I can trust your intervention and be helped.

And the truth is that this kind of person never really initiates being "against" anyone, unless that person is doing something to harm him or others. At that point, the person will take a stand to end the destruction, but even that kind of stand is against the destructiveness. There is a big difference between a wolf and a loving German shepherd who sometimes growls to protect someone. It's the difference between a predator and a loyal pet. The person of integrity only goes "against" someone who is destroying something good, and then is only against the destruction and not the person himself. If at all possible, he will only pin him down or restrain him until further help arrives, as opposed to injuring or killing.

## A Person of Grace

There are many ways to explain the above dynamics. Some think of it in terms of "altruism" or "love." Philosophy, psychology, and theology have all talked about it over millennia. We all have different ways of describing it, and we all know it when we see it. But of all these descriptions, my favorite word for this kind of character is *grace*.

We are familiar with this term in many ways, from having a "grace" period when we don't mail the check in on time, to hearing it in hymns or descriptions of exceptional people. The usage that I like the best is a theological one with the definition "unmerited favor." Grace is when we extend "favor" to someone, not because they have earned it in some way, but because we just possess it to give. It is a stance in life, a way of being. A "person of grace" is one who does the things we have described above of being "for" and not "against," and treating others in the way that she would want to be treated. It makes for ultimate trust.

So, if you want to leave the best wake possible, leave behind a trail of people who have experienced your being "for them." I heard a man describe his boss one time this way: "She was a tough one, but I always felt she wanted me to do well. She wanted me to win, even when she was hard on me." People of grace leave others better off than how they found them, even when they were getting nothing in return.

## Unmerited Help

In leadership, this means that you are for your people to do well, and to become all that they can be. It also means that you do things "for" them that are "unmerited" and help them get there. That does not mean, as we will see, that you do not have requirements and standards of performance for everyone in your life. But, what it does mean is that you will make efforts to help them to reach those standards. A leader with grace realizes that to reach the high standards she sets for her people may require that she provide coaching or training or encouragement or other resources to help them get there. They did not "earn" those things, and they are "unmerited." But, they serve to help them to reach the standard that is there. *Leaders without grace set the demand and do nothing to help people meet it.* Then, when they don't, they turn on them as adversaries.

A parent of grace works the same way. To achieve is the child's responsibility, but to empower the child is the parent's responsibility. So, instead of just setting a standard, the parent of grace gives support, coaching, teaching, structure, modeling, help, and consequences to empower the child to get there. Those are things that the child cannot provide and so are "unmerited." They are given without their being earned, and that is grace. But, grace is not removing the standard. The requirement stays, and the person of grace does what is possible to be "for" the other person's meeting it.

In marriage or intimate relationships, this kind of character does the same thing. Certainly one holds requirements and standards. But, if the other person does not meet them, the person of character does not retaliate or go instantly looking for someone who can. Instead, he or she becomes a redemptive force, to do good "for" the other person by providing "unmerited" or undeserved help. This may be by asking "How can I help you?" or calling a counselor in, or using other friends that have redemptive leverage, all the way to an intervention, as mentioned above. But the key is that this kind of person keeps the standard, while at the same time trying to be a **force** that helps the other person meet the standard. That is a trustworthy character that we can throw in with and depend on for the long haul.

Integrity, the kind that meets the demands of reality, is character that can handle another person's not being all someone needs that person to be. By moving as a positive force that is "for" the other person's getting better, as opposed to moving against him or disengaging because he isn't, the person leverages him to a higher level. As a result, these people do not get dragged down by other people's failures, but are a force of redemption in any situation, bringing it to a higher level. That translates into a relationship being healed in one's personal life, or a company getting turned around in one's business life. Either way, his or her character has been a force "for" the good of the other, even when no one made her do it. And that is why when you look at the long-term wake of this kind of person, you find long-term, successful relationships and work scenarios. When troublesome realities came along, his or her character was able to meet those demands and be a redemptive force.

# building trust
# through vulnerability

**f**or trust to work, there is a tricky power component. Think about it for a second. How much do you trust someone who is powerless? A wimp? Incompetent? Maybe you trust these people not to lie to you, but what aspects of your life would you "entrust" to them for safekeeping? Or to make better for you? When you buy insurance, for example, you don't get it from a kiosk at the flea market. You get it from one of those really tall buildings that looks as if it has been there awhile and isn't going anywhere. You want it from the "Rock," or some other symbol of strength and stability. Trust has a requirement of strength and power. Kids, for example, feel secure with a strong parent, and lost without one. Couples stay in love when their partner is strong enough to respect and depend on.

But, on the other side, if people are so strong that they are impenetrable in some way, or even so much stronger than we are, there is too much of a gap to bridge between the hearts. We can't identify with them enough to think they will understand us. They are too much "unlike" us for us to trust them, so we hold back and instead talk to people who do not seem to be so "otherworldly" that they can't relate to us humans. For trust to work in human relationships of any kind, whether leadership, marriage, parenting, or business, we have to be able to see some kind of crack in the armor so we feel that the other person is real. We might fear someone of great power or even admire him, but trust is another issue. In this way, therefore, we see a *tension in the dynamic of power and trust:*

> Not enough power, and we can't entrust things
> of value to the person. Too much power,
> and we can't feel that they could ever understand
> or relate to our own vulnerability.

For someone's character to be able to negotiate reality, there must be this dynamic tension between power and vulnerability. I remember one time when my mom did this successfully. She had a bumpy reality to negotiate with me when I was in the sixth grade. I had gotten mononucleosis and had some complications that led to my having to go into a hospital two hundred miles from where we lived for over a month. As a result, I had missed so much school that it was questionable whether I would be able to make it all up. But, when I returned, everyone gave it a try.

Not very long into it, I was not doing well. The fatigue that goes with that illness, coupled with whatever the workload was, plus being out of step with my classmates and friends, was all too much. I did not want to keep going and remember strongly feeling that I just couldn't climb this mountain. At that point, putting myself in my mother's shoes as a parent, she was in a crisis. I am sure that she felt the pressure of trying to get me to continue and push through so I would not lose an entire year of school, have to repeat a grade, be in a whole different class and set of friends, and be labeled a failure. Not to overdramatize the crisis involving an eleven-year-old, but sometimes being a parent can feel as if you were JFK negotiating the Bay of Pigs. I am sure my mother felt the heat, knowing that all of that hung in the balance.

It came to a head one morning as I was getting ready to go to school to face one more day of no energy, heavy demands to stay after school and catch up with old work and stay current with new assignments, being alone and out of step, and feeling like an outcast. While getting dressed, I just stopped and froze, shirt half-buttoned. In a little bit of a zombielike state, I was just standing there for what seemed like a long time, thinking about it all and at the same almost unable to think or move. It all felt so heavy. After standing there for who knows how long, my mother walked in.

"Get ready. You have to go to school," she said, trying to move me along.

"I don't want to go. I don't want to do this anymore. I can't do it."

And for some reason, I will never forget what happened next, as small as it seems. She just put her arm around me and said, "I know. Sometimes I don't want to go to work either, when I feel that way."

The world kind of stopped for a moment. "What?" I asked. "You feel like you don't want to go to work sometimes?"

"Sure. Sometimes when I am sick or don't feel well, it just is too much, and I don't want to go either."

"But you do. . . ."

She just nodded.

All I know is that at that point, something had shifted inside. I was still as tired, overwhelmed, and sick as I had been when I was frozen. But, for some reason, suddenly I felt as if I could do it. I felt transmuted inside from overwhelmed and unable, to overwhelmed and able. Courage, perseverance, and hope had somehow been created through that interaction.

She had given me her courage, perseverance, and strength to identify with, and use. When I say "transmuted," that is exactly what happened. *Transmuted* is a term that means that something is changed in form, substance, or nature. In this instance, one emotional state, and also a character state, was transmuted or "changed" to another through an interaction and connection. The technical aspects of how that happens are for psychologists and quantum physics to grapple with, but the reality aspects are available to people every day who have to "meet the demands of reality." People's emotional, intellectual, and character states can be changed as they connect with each other. And when you are in any significant relational context, from leadership, to marriage, to parenting, or others, you will hit moments where someone needs "transmutation" from you. That is a reality that will make a demand on your character. Do it well, and you build trust.

If your character is integrated, as we have defined it here, you will be able to take an eleven-year-old from losing a year of his life to catching up. You will be able to take a company or a department from losing all of its assets to making a profit. You will be able to keep someone you love from leaving the relationship. Or you will just be able to help those that are in your path. In any case, if you can connect in a way that gives other people something that they can use, you will do well. That is a big part of what leaders, teachers, parents, managers, and coaches do every day. But to do that, we have to build trust and connection through the keyhole of the *power balance* we are talking about.

What occurred there with my mom is that my executive functions, the things inside that I needed to "get it done," were inaccessible to me at that moment. My abilities to utilize my strength, initiative, and talents were not within my reach, which is exactly what discouragement is. An emotional state overwhelms one's abilities to solve the problem and keep going. You need the "courage" to use your abilities, and also some way to find them again. And in that state, the discouraged heart and the executive abilities are not connected, as if the wiring cannot reach between the two. So, the parts of me that I needed were unavailable to me. I could not find them. I was discouraged and could not find my abilities to go on and get it done.

So, my mother brought the two together. Where I was split, she was integrated, and connecting with her character integration brought mine together. I was split between my overwhelming feelings and my true abilities to go on. They could not hook up, so my discouragement left me powerless. But, she comes along and says, "I am sick sometimes and don't want to go either, *and* I do." That is character integration. It was not that she was feeling awful and did not go, or feeling fine and did go. She was both feeling bad *and* went. She brought them together, the overwhelmed and the able.

What that did for me was integrate my discouragement, my sickness and despair, with the abilities and strength that I had. Now my overwhelmed parts had some help. They were connected with my strengths. I could go forward and get it done. I had been transmuted.

The other aspect of this has to do with another process, called internalization. What that means is that we actually receive from other people what we do not possess in ourselves. *Encourage* literally came from "in courage." The courage is put "into" you from the outside. Our character and abilities grow through internalizing from others what we do not possess in ourselves. My mother literally "gave me strength" as if through a transfusion.

But, that could not have happened if she had just come along and said, "Oh, don't be afraid. You can do it," or, "It's not that hard," for neither of those would have integrated both sides of things. For me to be helped, and to connect with her, I needed a model who was *strong enough to depend on, but vulnerable enough to identify with.* That combination is what made it work. In essence, it said, *"Hey, she is like me, in that she is afraid sometimes and feels like she can't do it. But, she does it anyway. She pushes forward."*

> Her vulnerability is what made
> her power available to me.

That is the key point about character in this particular dimension. For you to build trust with people, you have to be vulnerable enough for them to identify with you, so that you are not so "unlike" them as to be alien. And, you have to be strong enough for them to feel that they can depend on you.

Research shows that models who are followed, which ultimately means trusted, are models who have the following characteristics:

1. They possess strength.
2. They possess "likeness" to the ones following them.
3. They are warm.
4. They are imperfect, and coping models, as opposed to perfect ones.

These are all bridges of both power and vulnerability, having to do with character. If a leader, for example, is weak, people lose faith. We do not follow incompetent leaders, for we do not feel that we can trust them with our lives or futures. Interestingly, strength here is about executive power, or ability, not force. A domineering, forceful person is not trusted as much as a person who displays strength through the exhibition of competent performance. Some of the weakest leaders are the ones who try to dominate through forcefulness of personality, as opposed to the ones who lead through the strength of their effectiveness. Being effective is experienced by others as strength.

"Likeness" has to do with having points that we can identify with that make the person more like me than alien to me. This is the reason that, in a political campaign, commercials show the candidate as a husband or wife, father or mother, or out throwing a football at a picnic or taking a walk in the park with kids or friends. We see that he or she is a regular person, and everyone feels more comfortable with trusting him, or her. The "stranger" anxiety goes down as we see that the candidates are more "like" us than different. As a result, we can connect with them and at the same time want to follow their strengths.

"Warm" means that their basic feel toward others is positive and kind. People who are cold, aloof, and feel unapproachable create a connection vacuum that can break down trust. We saw this from the Michael Dell feedback in the earlier chapter. But, when he began to open up, he seemed more like his employees and more approachable than before, and trust was rebuilt.

And "imperfect" means that they don't always get it right. They make mistakes and have faults. But, "coping" means that they face those directly and deal with them and overcome them. In that way, they are integrating imperfection with problem solving and overcoming, and that gives people a point with which to both identify and be inspired by.

As you can see, this takes a real, authentic person. If people are really narcissistic or have a need to be seen as more than they really are, or to be admired as having it all together, then they cannot be followed and trusted by others. The gap is simply too far to connect with. Or if they try to dominate others, bully them around, and be more "powerful" through sheer force, trust is not building. Compliance may be occurring, but ultimately, we move away from people that we are simply complying with. But with those we trust, we follow and throw in everything to give them the best we have.

I remember giving a talk one time in a corporation, and I gave an example of how I had once blown one of the very concepts I was teaching. At the end, a man walked up to me and said, "This was really helpful. But I have to admit, I was really skeptical and wasn't letting much of it get to me for a while. I figured, 'What does this guy know about my real world that I live in? He figures all this theory stuff is so simple.' Then, you told that story about how you have screwed it up too, and I suddenly felt like I could trust what you were saying. You had been there. So, I started listening, and I learned some good stuff. This is going to help me. But I never would have taken it in if you had not shown how you have had to learn too."

The boss, leader, parent, or friend who can be vulnerable enough to show that he or she has felt similar things and has made it through or overcome in some way is the one who gains our trust.

## Trust Through Need

Another powerful aspect of vulnerability that builds trust is the expression of need. When people feel needed, they perform at levels past the ones that come out of other requirements. To have a job or meet some quota is one thing. But to be performing because someone needs you takes you to levels that only the heart can push you to. There is a huge difference between the kind of leader who comes in and says, "Here are the goals. They have come down from above, and corporate is demanding that we get it done. So, no slacking off or not giving less than one thousand percent. Meet these numbers or I guarantee you some heads are going to roll. I will see to it personally. Anybody who doesn't do their part might as well get the résumé ready" versus "OK, guys. We have some big goals here. They are daunting, in some ways. But, that is what is being asked of us.

"Let me tell you something. I think we can do it, but I can't do it without you. I am going to need each and every one of you. Joe, without your brain, I won't be able to figure out what these numbers are saying. I need you to run your tightest analysis. And, Jen, I need that part of you that can sell heat to a desert. We won't get there without your pouring it on like only you can. And, Patty, I really am going to need you to run interference with the supply chain. It is going to be chaos, and if I have them breathing down my neck while I am trying to get the development done. . . . But, if you guys can give me all of that, we can get there."

Much is written about the "transparent" leader. In my experience, the best ones have a balance of transparency, in the ways we are discussing here. They are transparent in that they let the reality of where they are and the situations be known. We can only ultimately trust people who are being real with us. But part of that is transparency not just about the facts, but about themselves as well. We need to see their vulnerabilities, and how they are feeling about things. We also need to know about their failures, and times when they haven't gotten it right. That helps us to follow them.

One of the greatest things a mentor or manager can do is to sit down with someone who is struggling with the task and say, "Let me tell you about a situation I had when I was in your position. I blew it so bad that I didn't know how I ever would recover. Then . . ." To show that kind of reality gives courage to the person as they see you now, to know that you made it and yet it wasn't always that way.

But, again, the balance is key. The tension between vulnerability and strength in leaders cannot be lost. If a leader or a parent is using those she is trying to lead as a primary support group, and drawing from them her own sustenance, then things are topsy-turvy. Vulnerability is good, but to lead, one must also not be dependent on those he is leading. That kind of dependency and healing must come from somewhere else. Michael Dell might have had a therapist or consultants to work through his shyness, not his employees. What he did with them was to show that he was human, and at the same time able to keep performing. That is the kind of vulnerability that builds trust.

# III

# CHARACTER DIMENSION TWO

## Oriented Toward Truth

# 7

## in touch with reality

there is an old story about a dog food company that hit hard times. Sales were bad, and not getting better. The CEO had begun the company and was very attached to its performance. When things were going the wrong way, he was not happy. Being the decisive type that he was, he decided to take action. So, he fired the outside advertising firm that did all of the national campaigns.

The company geared up for the new branding push, new packaging, a new look, and even a new model on the bag. Certainly great things were in store. But, when the numbers came in, they were about the same. The CEO was more angry. Another inept advertising firm had failed him. What to do? "Get rid of them and find me a good one this time!" he ordered his team. "No more losers. We are spending too much in advertising to let this happen again!"

They moved quickly, hired the best, and launched with great expectations. Certainly this one would do the trick. New displays in retail space, samples left in pet stores and on doorsteps, treats given out at parks where people walk their dogs. No stone was left unturned in the dog world. They were going to know about this food. No dog left behind.

Then, the first quarter returns came in with the new thrust. No gains. Sales were the same. The CEO made another move, this time more drastic. He fired his marketing department and replaced them with the best and the brightest. Now finally, all the incompetence was eliminated. No more losers inside or outside the company. A new start.

The new team put together the new plan and executed it viciously. When the numbers came in, no one was happy. They were basically the same as they had been for the previous few years. No gains. The CEO called a meeting. He wanted to know who was responsible for this. Someone was not doing his job, he said, and he wanted to know who. Find him and get me someone who can make this work was his message.

Right in the middle of the meeting as he was breaking down delivery schedules in supply chains, space allocation in stores, demographics, and pricing of the advertising focus and other execution issues, a young, somewhat quiet, nonassuming little manager raised his hand. "Sir, may I say something?" he asked.

"Yes, Jones. What is it?" the CEO inquired, a little thrown off by this interruption.

"Sir . . . the dogs don't like it," Jones said.

The room was quiet for what seemed like a long time as the CEO just looked at Jones. What happened next is the subject of this aspect of character.

## An Orientation Toward Truth: 101

As we saw earlier, whenever the discussion of "integrity" comes up, the default position is to talk about honesty and ethics. As we also saw, that is certainly an aspect of the foundation, as without it there can be nothing else. If someone is an outright liar or cheat, then there is nowhere to go with him. As Jack Welch said in *Winning,* firing that kind of person is a "no-brainer." If everyone had that basic honesty, we would not have had the scandals that rocked Wall Street in the huge meltdowns of Enron et al. "Telling the truth" is the first part of having an orientation toward truth. We all desire to be with honest people.

The sad reality, though, is that many people do lie. In fact, depending on how we define it, most of us do, at some time or another, in some form or other. "How are you feeling?" You say fine even though you are not. "How was my solo?" a friend asks you after the community concert, or the church service. "Great!" you say. "I enjoyed it." Really? Is that what you were thinking inside your head? Not always, yet we do it for a number of reasons. We sometimes want people to feel good, we don't want to hurt them, we don't want them to be mad at us, and many other factors cause us to fudge sometimes, at least at this level. But if all lack of truthfulness were at this level, we would probably be OK, other than to have less than stellar solos at times. More about when this gets to be a problem in chapter 10, embracing the negative.

Sadly, though, lying does not stop at that level. Many people of good character operate in this way: "I won't unnecessarily hurt someone's feelings (there is no good answer to the question 'Does this dress make me look fat?'), but I will **not** lie about real issues of fact." Those are the people we most like to deal with. But, in reality, some otherwise really good people *will* tell lies when it helps them. I once had an employee who was applying for a mortgage and wanted me to fudge on his salary level so he could get the loan. We both knew he could afford the payments, so there was no issue in reality, right? This person was basically an honest, trustworthy person interpersonally and in business, and yet this kind of "lying" seemed OK to him. I said no, even though there was not a "reality issue" about whether he could pay.

Although I might have been tempted to tell him that his singing sounded good, I was not going to tell an outright lie about something in fact. That is fraud and clearly wrong, and no matter how he felt about me afterward (I hoped it did not affect our relationship), I had no choice. It would have been a clear lie. But, many people do not see it that way. They feel that an occasional "fudging" is OK, if there is some good reason, and it won't hurt anybody. From taxes to giving excuses for not showing up, they lie.

Certainly there are some realities to situational ethics. If someone breaks in with a gun and asks if anyone else is in the office, most of us would be the first to tell them no, to protect the life of someone who was hiding under the desk. But that kind of moral reasoning is filtered through a hierarchy of the "greatest good" and gets complicated. Generally, the people who suffer over questions like that are people of good integrity anyhow, and we don't have to worry about them. They worry enough. Their interest is always to do the highest good, even if they get it wrong in some situations.

But in the situations where there is no supreme, moral reasoning that lends one to say less than is true, then we have to say that to have character integrity is to tell the truth, no matter the costs. In fact, truthfulness is really measured in terms of our tendency to tell it when it *hurts* in some way. People fudge or lie when there is a risk of some sort of loss or negative consequence. And that is where our study in character truthfulness begins.

"I did not have sexual relations with that woman, Ms. Lewinsky" is a quote that everyone recognizes. It was made, obviously, in light of impending loss or negative consequences. What if he had said, from the beginning, "I did a bad thing, and I am sorry." We would have probably seen a different wake. But, the tendency to hide the truth where there are potential consequences is a part of human nature, and sadly, *one that usually makes us incur more negative consequences than if we had told the truth.*

Working with couples over the years has shown me this reality over and over. I remember one woman sobbing in my office after finding out that the financial picture in her marriage was different from what her husband had led her to believe, for the hundredth time. He had been trying the best he could to make the money they needed, but it was not working. She was, understandably, not doing well with the ongoing financial insecurity, and his continued attempts to make it in his own business as opposed to working for someone else for a steady paycheck were not helping her to calm down, either. Start-ups are tough, as anyone knows, and some people are more vulnerable to that kind of shakiness. She was like that, and when there was a shortfall, she did not do well. She would react to him in excitable ways and get angry or upset that things were not as they "should be."

Slowly, as the process went on, he felt the pressure to keep her happy, as well as to get her off his case. Her anger and disappointment frightened him, so he would lead her to believe that things were better than they actually were, hoping that he could somehow make it all work and catch up before she found out. He was always robbing Peter to pay Paul, which means that he was juggling to make her feel secure, and to keep her from putting more heat on him.

But, the big problem here was not that he was juggling, *but that he was not telling her he was juggling.* There had been other times in their marriage when, to avoid her anger and disappointment, he had led her to believe things were better than they were. Then, when she found out the truth, he discovered what is one of the most difficult lessons to learn for those who fudge the truth to make other people happy or to avoid negative consequences:

The consequences of deceit are usually greater
than the ones of the truth.

She was sobbing in my office not because of the finances. She could have, and would have, dealt with the financial rocky road that they were on and worked it out. She was sobbing because, as she put it, she could not trust him. "I feel like I am standing on quicksand," she cried. "I think things are one way, and then I find out they are another. I can deal with the truth, but *I cannot deal with thinking one thing is true and then finding out that it has not been true all along.*"

The bigger consequence for him than her disappointment over the money was her loss of trust in the relationship and the reality of their lives. We can negotiate reality if we know what it is. But, when we are given something other than the truth, we are in trouble. She felt that awful insecurity every time he now said something to her. She had no reason to think that it was reality. For all she knew, if he said things were fine, the foreclosure notices were coming tomorrow.

Now, if you take her anxiety to Wall Street dimensions, you can see why investors fled the scene after the corporate accounting scandals in the last few years. Until the basic problem of truthfulness was more vigorously addressed, there was no way to trust. The issue is the same on Wall Street as it is in one's personal life: character integrity.

Basic truthfulness and reality 101, as we are calling it here, is that people of good character are people who can be trusted to tell the truth, and to *give a representation of reality to others as best as they understand it.* That is the foundation of all of life, from business, to government, to family, to commerce, to friendship. Without it, we don't have much. That is why some countries, for example, have such little economic hope. The corruption and lack of integrity at the basic levels is so rampant, no one can invest and do business there. It is foundational.

But, what does that have to do with dog food?

## Truth 201 and Above

If not lying and not fudging are the foundational aspects of having an orientation to reality, what comes after that? And what does it have to do with success? A lot.

The premise here is that telling the truth is foundational, but **not enough** for success in love and life. A lot of honest, nonfudging people are not reaching their potential, and not getting to the levels of performance and success that their brains and talents should be taking them. *And the reason is not that they are lying, but that they miss parts of reality that are important to making things work.* In the kind of successful character that we are talking about here, the integrated or "whole" character, a grasp of truth is always present and increasing, which requires some specific traits. We will look at those, but first, let's just make sure that we understand why this is so important.

If you are in the dog food business, you are not going to make money with the best dog food in the world if no one knows about it, as our CEO above reasoned. You have to have some way of marketing it and telling the world how to find it. Chances are that if you have no marketing ability, then by the time word of mouth got around the country, your capital costs would overtake the timeline and you would be out of business. You are better off if a lot of people know quickly in order to get to the critical mass, or "tipping point." So, if your marketing is poor, then you have to see that reality so you can fire the marketing person and get the job done.

But, what if the reality is that your marketing is the best in the world, but your *dog food is horrible?* Better marketing only gets you more disappointed dogs and actually puts you further behind than if you sold less, because your brand is getting trashed. They have tried you and moved on. Much better to know that your food tastes bad to Fido and fix that before you get it out to the world. Then, you are standing in and on reality, which is the only place that good things happen.

Or, even trickier, what if selling dog food to supermarkets is not where the real market is at all? *What if the world has changed, and you can't see it?* What if you have some blinders on and can't see the new drive-through, fast-food dog-store trend?

Or, even bigger, in one's personal life, what if the problem is not that your child's teacher is out to lunch, but your child is slipping into isolation and you are losing her and don't know it, and that is why her grades are suffering? Missing reality like that can have disastrous consequences in the areas we care about the most.

One of my favorite sayings is, no matter how difficult it is to hear,

Reality is always your friend.

The reason is almost a truism: everything else is a fantasy. So, for us to get real results in the real world, we *must be in touch with what is, not what we wish things were or think things should be or are led by others to believe they are. The only thing that is going to be real in the end is what is.* That is where profits are going to be made, and that is where love is going to be found.

In the book *Good to Great,* Jim Collins shares research on companies that transformed to greatness, outperformed the markets by

6.9 times, and sustained those results for fifteen years. These companies, which had a very real *wake,* had one factor that he referred to as Confront the Brutal Facts. This was the principle that success can only be built through seeing reality clearly and facing it. If the dogs don't like it, you need to put your arms around that. He puts it this way:

"The good-to-great companies displayed two distinct forms of disciplined thought. The first, and the topic of this chapter, is that they infused the entire process with the brutal facts of reality. You absolutely cannot make a series of good decisions without first confronting the brutal facts. The good-to-great companies operated in accordance with this principle, and the comparison companies generally did not" (p. 70).

His language comes from a quote in a conversation with Admiral Jim Stockdale, a prisoner of war in Vietnam, tortured and imprisoned for eight years, and awarded the Congressional Medal of Honor. In that conversation, Stockdale gives the secret of his survival:

"This is a very important lesson. You must never confuse faith that you will prevail in the end—which you can never afford to lose—*with the discipline to confront the most brutal facts of your current reality, whatever they might be*" (p. 85, italics mine).

Whether in a horrible POW camp, a conflict over the finances of a marriage, or a Fortune 500 company's strategy, meeting reality is always your friend. It will be your key to creating and getting to a new reality. But, you can't get there if you don't first know where you truly stand. As my marriage counselee put it, "I don't care what the truth is, just give it to me. I have to know what is real. Then I can know what to do."

High achievers face reality and deal with it. Those who don't, avoid reality in some way or have aspects to their character that keep them out of touch with it, as we shall see. Many times this is for comfort's sake. It is difficult to see what really is, and to live with it. We feel better when we can make it not so, in some form or fashion. We attribute the truth of our performance to some outside influence, as if to say, "It wasn't me." For some reason, the CEO could not see that it was not the marketing. It was the dog food. What in his makeup kept him from seeing that?

I grew up as a competitive golfer, and one of the best lessons I ever learned in life came from my childhood coach, a crusty, experienced pro. In my early teens, if I played in a tournament, I had to report to him and tell him how it went. He would ask me what I shot, and I would begin to editorialize. "Pro! I was really doing well and would have shot under par, until number sixteen. I hit it in a bare spot and it kicked right into that impossible rough. I couldn't get it out and made a double bogey. If that hadn't happened, I would have shot 69! After that, I lost my concentration and made two more bogeys." I could almost feel the excitement of my subpar round that had turned into a 73. But what I was feeding him was some false reality I was living off of, as if the 69 were more real than the 73. It felt a lot better, what "could have been . . . if only . . ."

I don't remember when he first said it, I only remember that he *always* said it until he did not have to say it anymore because I got it: "Henry, I didn't ask you *how?* I asked you *how many?*" In other words, the **scorecard doesn't care** how you got this and that kind of bad break, and how you could almost have played well, and how if the earth were square, you would somehow be Jack Nicklaus. By his simple mantra, he was saying to me, *reality is what you shot.* How many strokes did it take you, period? That is what is true, and as long as you hang out in what you wish were true, or how you think it should be true, you will never see what *is* true and never get to where you could get.

But, when I learned that, I had to see what was real. I *did* hit it in the rough, and I *did* bogey two more holes. I *did* blow the round.

Now, deal with that. Face the swing habits that caused that, work them out, and the next time you will have a chance to make things different. But not until you realize that you shot 73, not 69, or whatever you wish were true.

My client was using this same mental process with his wife, and many of Collins's examples of companies that failed used it as well: *spending time in some alternate universe that does not exist to make the one that we are living in feel better.* But, in reality, we can make the one we live in better only by seeing what is going on there and dealing with it head-on. As Collins points out, that is where success can be achieved, and it is not out of people's grasp, when they face reality. When you think about it, there is a simple reason: things happen for a reason.

I was talking to a successful person in publishing about books that do well, and why. That got us to a conversation about people who do well, and why. Toward the end of the conversation, he said, "In the end, people get to where they are supposed to. If they make it, there was a reason. If they don't, there was one too."

I knew what he was referring to. While there are exceptional strokes of luck and circumstances that grace people's lives, and awful tragedies that hit others and affect outcomes, the general rule is that you can usually look at some scenario and see "why."

It is a lot like gravity and an airplane. It is not luck that it stays in the air. If it is up there, and still flying, then the wings are on pretty straight, and the engine is putting out power. The jets are not on fire. If it is in the air, there is a reason. Those are the kinds of realities that govern this universe. Despite chaos theory, and antinomies of randomness that emerge into order, and all other kinds of strange things we don't understand, there is still order to the universe and reality rules. The trick is to find it and get in step with it, as random or ordered as it may or may not be. What it is, is what it is. And the successful people live in it and negotiate it.

But to do that, we first have to *see*. What keeps us from seeing that it is not the marketing, but the dog food?

Reality 201 and higher is for those who are honest. They have the foundation and do not lie. But, they also have other character aspects to who they are that keep them from having blind spots way past lying. Our dog-food CEO was not a liar. He was just out of touch. And here is the point: the things that cause that to happen are rooted in character. We will now take a look at what some of those things past basic honesty are. What is it about some people's character that helps them see and be in touch with more of reality than others? What gives them clear vision? Let's see.

# what people in touch look like

**p**astor Rick Warren made publishing history when *The Purpose Driven Life* became the biggest-selling hardback nonfiction book in the history of publishing. He has achieved incredible things both in publishing and in building a successful church and organization. The church that he began, Saddleback, has eighty thousand people on its rolls.

But it was not always that way. In 1980, when he and his wife, Kaye, penniless and fresh out of seminary, moved to Southern California to begin a church, he took an interesting approach. Instead of the usual path of finding a facility, getting some musicians, and preparing some sermons, his first move was not to begin it at all. What he did, instead, was go door-to-door and ask people why they didn't go to church. Then, he built a church that had none of those reasons. And he gave them what they needed. Today, Saddleback is one of the largest churches in America. As *Forbes* put it, "Were it a business, Saddleback church would be compared with Dell, Google, or Starbucks" (2/16/04).


## Seeking Reality

Now, what does that have to do with character? Think about it. Warren did not, *assume or think or act as if* he knew what reality was. Instead, he *sought it.* He went looking for it, even door-to-door. But, many people because of pride or narcissism, or just bullheadedness, approach a task like that and basically say, "Get out of my way. I know what I am doing." They have a know-it-all approach and, as a result, miss what reality truly is.

The people who see reality as their friend, however, do not assume that they have a grasp on it. I have written the story elsewhere of a friend of mine who was Global VP of Marketing for Procter and Gamble, and had great success in two continents, when he was sent to China to develop the business from a small beginning. In two years, he took it from near nothing to close to a billion dollars in sales. It was an incredible accomplishment. I asked him one day how he did it.

You really don't know what you don't know. When you think that everyone thinks that teeth are teeth, you find out something different, if you are looking for reality. He went there and first tried to understand the people. He lived on a rice farm to find out how they used detergent and also to learn as much about the people as possible. Then he found out something else about them that led to huge profits:

"I learned that Chinese people believed teeth were a solid enamel and pretty much impervious to damage. This made tooth brushing more of a 'clean the surface off' project. Chinese tooth-pastes had lots of suds and good taste, but only one or two inconsequential local brands had fluoride. Colgate with fluoride had been launched three years ahead of us, so we had a real disadvantage. In contrast to this 'established consumer belief,' when we showed Chinese people that their teeth were actually really porous with thousands of little holes, and that Crest fluoride actually filled in and strengthened their teeth, we saw strong and lasting consumer response to the brand."

What accomplished that? Character. It was his character that did not assume he knew it all, but as accomplised as he was, still had more to learn. He went there to find out what he did not know, and learned the reality he needed to know in the process.

He had the humility to go in and not assume that he had it all figured out and instead to *seek to find out what reality was.* People who have an orientation to the truth *seek it out.* They look for it and do everything they can to find it so that they know where to stand, what steps to take, etc. They basically see reality as their best ally, so finding it becomes of utmost importance.

The interesting thing about this kind of people is the hunger that they have for finding out what is true. They are different from people who are honest but do not take active steps to find out more of what reality is. A lot of people are not in denial when reality comes and knocks on their door. They are able to acknowledge it and not resist it. But, they are basically passive about it, not active. The kind of people I am talking about here go after reality as if their lives depend on it. They *have* to find it.

In the Michael Dell example earlier, no one just came up to him and told him that half of his employees were ready to leave. That reality came from seeking it. They did internal interviews to find out where people were, and how they felt about being there. That is the kind of seeking that I am referring to, and it is important in all aspects of life. Marriages that do well, for example, have partners who are constantly seeking out the reality of where the other person is. In John Gottman's research, for example, he found that in strong marriages the partners are very aware of the reality of the other's world:

"In contrast, emotionally intelligent couples are intimately familiar with each other's world. I call this having a richly detailed love map—my term for that part of your brain where you store all the relevant information about your partner's life. Another way of saying this is that these couples have made plenty of cognitive room for their marriage. They remember the major events in each other's history, and they keep updating their information as the facts and feelings of their spouse's world change."

And later: "Couples who have detailed love maps of each other's world are far better prepared to cope with stressful events and conflict" (John M. Gottman, Ph.D., and Nan Silver, *The Seven Principles for Making Marriage Work* [Three Rivers Press: NY, 1999]).

These couples "keep updating their information as the facts and feelings of their spouse's world change," meaning they actively seek reality about each other. In other words, knowing reality in both business and marriage is the first step in making it all work. But this kind of knowledge does not come passively. It has to be actively sought.

The opposite of actively seeking reality is avoidance. The person who avoids finding out what is true may be doing that for a variety of character reasons. Take our dog-food CEO. In his avoidance of seeing that his product had some major problems, he lost a lot of money, manpower, time, and market share. Why would he be so blind? It seems simple to us as we hear the story, but every day, people do the same kinds of things out of basic character problems. Here are a few of the most common examples:

- Emotional investment in some other reality—let's say the CEO's dad had started the company and come up with the

original formula for the food. To say that it was not good
would mean letting go of a lot of emotional history.

● Fear of dealing with the ramifications—if the product is
bad, then where are we? Are we even in business anymore?
If that is our main formula, and it is horrible, what's next?
This kind of reality calls for some courage to possibly face
starting over and finding a whole new way to make it work.

Basic pride, omnipotence, arrogance, grandiosity, or narcissism—
this is the person who sees himself as above others, better than
everyone else, knowing all things, and in touch with all reality. To
admit that he is wrong about something does not even come up on
the screen.

Whatever the fears or reasons, it is about someone's basic
makeup. An orientation to the truth is a stance that people take in
life. It is the way that they are on the planet or, as the existentialists
said, their way of "being in the world." They lean into truth and reality as a direction in life, the way a compass points north. It is the
way they are.

This seeking for truth tends to be balanced in three directions,
also. First, they seek it about the **external world**. They want to know
what is true around them, in their company, in the market, and in
the universe. They want to be intimate with the ways that things
are. They know that that is the only way to ultimately succeed, and
they have given up the pride of "already knowing what is" in ex-
change for the profit of finding out what truly is. As Peter Drucker
says:

"One constant theme is, therefore, the need for the decision
maker in the individual enterprise to face up to reality and resist the
temptation of what 'everybody knows,' the temptations of the cer-
tainties, of yesterday, which are about to become the deleterious su-
perstitions of tomorrow. To manage in turbulent times, therefore,

means to face up to the new realities. It means starting with the question: 'What is the world really like?' rather than with the assertions and assumptions that made sense only a few years ago" (Peter F. Drucker, *The Daily Drucker* [Harper Business 2004]).

Second, they seek this kind of feedback about **themselves**. They don't only wait for others to give them feedback, they also go after it themselves. They desire it and see it as an opportunity to grow. I was doing an executive retreat one time with a small group of CEOs who had gathered for three days to process things. One of them was an up-and-comer in the industry, a rising star. The rest of the group had been around longer and had more experience. On the first night, they all went around the group and shared where they were, what they were up to, how they were doing it, and what they needed to get from the group.

When he finished, one of the more experienced guys looked up and said, "Want some feedback?" He said it in a way that left you wondering whether he was going to give sage advice or rail at the young man for being out to lunch in some way. There was just no way to tell from his poker face. But I will never forget the young superstar's immediate response: "By all means. Give me a gift." He saw the feedback, whatever it was, as a gift because it could give him some reality that he did not know. I remember thinking, "We will be watching this guy's accomplishments for a long time."

The good ones want to know the reality of who they are and are in tune with the fact that we do not see ourselves accurately. They "seek" out this knowledge in a variety of ways. Some commission 360-degree feedback projects to see how they are doing. Others submit themselves to a mentor, accountability group, therapist, or someone else who has a good view of them. But, when they do, they are not looking for flattery. They are looking for reality. They ask others to tell them what they see.

If you want to know your comfort level in this matter, think of going to the people you work with or are in close personal relationships with and give them 100 percent permission to be totally honest with you in answering this question: "What is it like to be on the other end of me?" Some will get exhilarated at the prospect of finding out more about themselves, while others will get nervous even at the idea. The one who is a seeker is usually excited by the prospect, seeing that kind of reality as a friend. Even if it means facing up to some painful news, he or she sees the result as positive.

Only through finding out this kind of reality do we know our true strengths and weaknesses. Top performers rely on that knowledge. They major in their strengths and protect themselves from their weaknesses. But without knowing reality about ourselves, we often don't even know what those are. And knowing one's strengths and weaknesses can be the difference between success and failure. As Marcus Buckingham and Donald Clifton, from the Gallup Organization, put it:

> *You will excel only by maximizing your strengths, never by fixing your weaknesses. This is not the same as saying "ignore your weaknesses." The people we described did not ignore their weaknesses. Instead, they did something much more effective. They found ways to manage around their weaknesses, thereby freeing them up to hone their strengths to a sharper point. Each of them did this a little differently. Pam liberated herself by hiring an outside consultant to write the strategic plan. Bill Gates did something similar. He selected a partner, Steve Ballmer, to run the company, allowing him to return to software development and rediscover his strengths' path. Sherie, the dermatologist, simply stopped doing the kind of medicine that drained her. Paula, the magazine editor, turned down job offers* (Buckingham and Clifton, Now, Discover Your Strengths [Free Press, 2001], *pp. 26–27).*

The winners are the ones who know themselves accurately and can build on that knowledge. They can utilize their strengths and "manage around their weaknesses." In my view, these kinds of weaknesses are not the kinds of character issues we are talking about, but areas of nongiftedness. Character is always to be both managed and "fixed." But all along the path, as we are growing toward wholeness, we really need to know the truth of "what is." The more we know about ourselves, the stronger our position.

When you think about it, it is the people who have little self-awareness (see below) who are the most dysfunctional. It is a paradox of life that the less we look at our shortcomings, the more others do. The extent that we are in denial is usually the extent to which others are staring at us, saying, "What is his problem?" The less we look at ourselves, the more others have to.

The key here, though, is that human nature is to "not look." From the fig leaf in the story of the Garden of Eden, to Freud's concepts of defense mechanisms, to Shakespeare, to existential and humanistic psychology's concepts of the "false-self," hiding the truth from ourselves is a trait of humanity that no one really disputes. As Shakespeare put it, "The fool doth think he is wise, but the wise man knows himself to be a fool" (*As You Like It*). The fool is out of touch, not only with his own foolish parts, or "weaknesses," but also with his strengths as well. The natural human tendency is to not face ourselves as we really are.

But, the wise character does face himself or herself. Herein is the problem: If we delude ourselves, how then shall we see ourselves, since the "observer" (us) is deluded? The answer is in this character trait of "seeking" truth from the outside. The winners ask. They sometimes hire people to help them see it. They value feedback from others about themselves, knowing that they themselves have blind spots. Michael Dell had to hear it from others. From his perspective, he was shy. From theirs, he was aloof. But he won when he sought out information from the outside.

If we are afraid of the truth about ourselves and have a character "stance" to hide, then we are headed in the wrong direction, away from reality. Think of the character issues that get in the way and create this kind of fear:

- Fear of seeing that I am wrong or have faults that are ugly. Those lead to guilt, or fears that I may lose love, approval, or standing with the people I care about.
- A fixed view of myself from past experience, either positive or negative. Our early relationships give us a view of who we are, and to look at new input means challenging those views, which leads to anxiety.
- A lack of skills or resources to deal with what I find. If I open Pandora's box, what will I do with it?
- A need for a total redo of a life plan or script. What if Mom or Dad made me believe that I was gifted in some area or should be able to do so and so, and the reality is that I am not? Now what? Or if this was my own dream, but I am out of touch with my true areas of giftedness?

The character who seeks reality about himself or herself has the courage to embrace whatever reality he finds. When we talk about "character that meets the demands of reality," part of that is meeting the demand of the truth about ourselves. The promise of that pain is that when we do that, we can meet the demands of the external world even better. The one who is true about herself is the one who is most able to negotiate things outside of herself as well.

Willow Creek Church in suburban Chicago was studied by Harvard Business School as a result of its incredible growth culture. From small beginnings, it has now become one of America's largest churches with twenty thousand attendees, and its leadership conferences have been host to presidents as well as highly esteemed business leaders in America. If you spend much time working in their culture, you will hear the phrase "give me the last ten percent." That means they know two things.

First, people tend to hold back on feedback that might be difficult for someone to hear and do not always express their full critique of someone's performance. They might, for example, say, "It was OK, not your best, but OK." But the part they are holding back, the last 10 percent, is "OK, if I am totally honest, you need to go back to the drawing board and start over." Or: "Before you ever do that again, get some help." Second, *we need the last 10 percent to be the best that we can be.* I am convinced that one aspect of their huge success in reaching their goals has been to develop a culture of characters who desire to hear the last 10 percent.

To do that requires character hunger for the truth. Not only negative, but positive and neutral truth as well. We will talk later about embracing the negative realities in chapter 10, and more about the character issues that get in the way. But the issue here is that character of integrity has a *hungry seeking,* an *appetite,* to know the truth about itself. And that has to come from reaching to outside sources and being open to hearing it.

Sometimes it is even positive. Sometimes people ward off positive reality about themselves because it would mean a lot to take responsibility for it. "You have some gifts and some abilities that you have not been using, and we are going to promote you to head a division" may be frightening news for some. And they might ward it off or not see it, unless it breaks through from the outside. Left to their own self-appraisal, they may never take the growth step needed to become the person they could be. We avoid the truth sometimes in both directions, positive and negative. The winners seek both, even the kind that would stretch them out of their comfort zone.

And third, they seek the truth about **other people.** Not only do we avoid seeing reality about ourselves, but sometimes because of past experiences, and sometimes to keep our own internal stability, we do not see others in the reality of who they are.

Recall our leader in chapter 2, Brad? He could not see the reality of Rick, his VP of sales. He could not see clearly who the guy was, his strengths and weaknesses. That was not because of some niceness à la Mr. Rogers, who would never assume anything negative about anyone. It was, instead, rooted in his dependency on Rick for his own performance. He was not trying to be a good guy and give someone a pass. He was trying to save himself. As a result, he was doing himself in by not facing the truth about another person.

From the lonely individual who falls in love with a nutcase—even when his or her friends are saying, *"What are you thinking?"*—to people who make bad hires in business or forge bad partnerships, our tendency to distort others is a big part of how we run into trouble. And we typically do it for a few reasons that have to do with our makeup.

First, we are blind to correctly seeing others who somehow remind us of unresolved figures from our past. You have heard this referred to as transference. It is our tendency to see others through the lens of people from previous experience. In a good way, it can cause us to be more attuned to things that others might miss, in that we can be vigilant in seeing hurtful patterns that we may have grown up with. But, if we have never worked those through, it can cause us either to be blind to them or to overreact when we are faced with them. Almost everyone can relate to this experience, in that we have more difficulty with a certain kind of person than others. Yet, other people may just experience that person as having a quirk and are able to work around it. But it gets us off course because of unresolved hurt or issues with a person like that from our history.

Second, we distort them out of our own needs. That was the

Brad and Rick example. Or the lonely person who needs a relation-ship so badly that anyone looks good. Or if we are feeling over-whelmed, for example, we might idealize people who present a lot of strength. They give us a secure feeling in all of the chaos. What we miss is that they might be bulldozers and insensitive to people's needs. The love for the strength wears off and we are left with a jerk. Or, the opposite can happen. If you have recently been through a period of getting beat up by the bulldozers, then you are really drawn to a person with some people sensitivity. But, you miss that in their niceness they are overly passive, and you lose respect for them soon after the initial relief wears off.

Third, we distort them sometimes because we are not in touch with something about ourselves. I remember a client of mine one time just railing on irresponsible people and deceivers. They just drove him crazy. And some of the people he would label that way were really not bad. They might have a few quirks, but they were not irresponsible or deceptive. But he had them labeled that way. I remember thinking that he was seeing them in such a distorted way, and yet when I would confront it, he would have nothing to do with what I was saying.

After a while, though, others who worked around him came for-ward with some truth about him that he had not been disclosing. He was not paying attention to many of his responsibilities and was deceiving people all along the way into thinking things that were misrepresentations. In psych parlance, he was "projecting." He was projecting onto others what he was blind to in himself. As a result, he was not seeing reality in them and was missing a lot of good peo-ple along the way. He could not see their good parts because he was projecting onto them his own faults.

I remember one leader who was about to give away the store to hire a guy because of this guy's "amazing strengths" in a particular area. When I interviewed the second guy as part of my coaching him, I could not believe how the leader had idealized this guy's strengths. He was nowhere as "awesome" as my client described him. But what was more surprising was that the very abilities that my client was seeing in this guy and about to pay dearly for were abilities that *he himself had, but could not own.* They were not part of his self-image. He projected his own strengths onto this other guy because he was not owning them. He did not need to hire him at all. He needed to see that he was capable of doing everything he was about to hire someone to do. He needed to take a growth step past the self-image that he had developed in a relationship with a father and a brother who always put him down.

In contrast, people of integrated character tend to delude themselves less about others. They have worked through their own issues and distortions about other people to a degree that they can see pretty clearly. And, as a part of that, they seek to know more. Wise people are "cautious in friendship," as the proverb says. They seek to get to know a person clearly, as the person truly is, before they hire him, marry him, become partners with him, *or* divorce him, fire him, or not go forward with him. *We can be off in either direction, and the complete character is always asking, "Is this me, or him?"* They are checking to see where the perception is coming from and trying to find out what is true. We have all heard both "I underestimated her" or "I overestimated her." People who have integrated their character tend to do both of those less because they are seekers of reality and desire to see it, even if it is going to be uncomfortable or make them deal with some things.

## The Observing Ego

We have seen the value of getting reality feedback from others in order to get a clear picture of ourselves. That is essential. Another feedback mechanism that we need is feedback about ourselves *from ourselves.* This is our ability to monitor our own thoughts, behaviors, attitudes, feelings, abilities, choices, values, desires, talents, and the like. It is one thing to drive safely when you look in the rearview mirror and there is a policeman. That is external feedback. It is another thing to drive safely when you are out on the road by yourself. That is maturity.

There are a lot of terms for this aspect of human makeup, but psychologists refer to it as the observing ego. *Ego* means "I," and *observing* means to "watch over" or "be attuned to" or "notice." So, it is the part of me that is watching me. And successful characters who leave the best wakes have a lot of this. They tend to see themselves as they are, and to observe their behavior as it is happening.

I left a strategic-planning retreat recently with a group that I am doing a publishing project with. At the end of the meeting things got a little sour. The problem was that the president of the company who was leading the meeting ran off in his own direction and agenda and left others behind, somewhat pushing his plan through and then talking as if it were everyone's. I could feel the atmosphere change and had some strong feelings myself about what had happened. Upon leaving, I wanted some time to think about how I was going to respond to what had occurred before talking to him. This was somewhat of a pattern with him, and I wanted to address the bigger picture. He was a good guy and someone I like working with, so resolving it in a good way mattered to me.

But before I got back to him, I received an e-mail that apologized for what had occurred, and that he was aware that he had "thrown cold water" on the meeting, as he put it. We later talked, and he shared his awareness of his tendency to do what he had done that day, and he said he wanted to talk further about it. He saw what he had done *before* it was mentioned to him. My hope for its not happening again went up. Character that sees itself is usually able to self-correct.

We all have issues, and our weird moments. But we do best when we are able to see them ourselves and correct them. Not only did this incident give me more confidence about our future, it also said something about why this man has risen to the ranks of CEO of a public company and been successful for so many years.

I remember another meeting I was in where the head of a major television network was talking and just stopped in the middle of what he was saying and said, "Forgive me if I am taking over here. I have a tendency to do that sometimes, so just let me know if I am talking too much. But I have a lot of thoughts about this." The rest of the room said, "No, no, go ahead. This is helpful," etc. But I was struck by the same trait, that of *instant* self-awareness. He knew his tendencies and how they could be disruptive and could see himself doing it there. The more we have that, the more we are like the best airplanes or spaceships. The instrument panel instantly tells the pilot if he is off course or running hot. As a result, corrections can be made before something bad happens.

Every human has faults, weaknesses, delusions, distortions, emotions that are not totally mature, lapses in judgment, and many other things that can cause problems. As we grow, those decrease as we mature, but we will always have some. That is inescapable. But, the *trouble that those things cause us is very escapable, to the degree that we can observe them.* When we can see ourselves and what we are doing, we can always do something about it. But, not until. The observing ego is one of the big keys to making anything work. The ability to ask oneself "What am I doing here?" is a compass that will keep things on the right track.

## "Neutralized Truth"

High achievers with good wakes also have another aspect to their character regarding truth. It has to do with what psychologists call the "emotional valence" to whatever truth we are dealing with. *Valence* has to do with the power of an emotionally loaded issue. Sometimes, when we are facing difficult things, the negative power of the emotions involved overcomes the ability to metabolize the reality itself. The extreme case would be something traumatic, whereby someone is overcome and unable to respond. But day to day, we all can identify with what happens when we face a hard piece of news at work and have to respond.

The characters who do well have an ability to "neutralize" hard truth, making it not overwhelming, but something to be looked at without all of the awful and terrible emotion that goes along with it. We will deal with this in more depth in the section where we talk about embracing the negative, but it is also important to mention it now as it is a key character block in some people's ability to see reality.

The idea here is not to turn everyone into a Mr. Spock, devoid of feeling. But people with integrated character are able to look at issues and problems regarding things other than themselves, or regarding themselves, or regarding others, in a way that the "sting" is taken out of them. They neutralize negative truth with kindness, for example. Or, they just are not harsh in the delivery of it. It is about the reality and not the person. They deal with the way things are and are able to see things in a way that is not personalized about them, or anyone else. That way they can eat reality for breakfast without getting sick. When they see an issue, they deal with it without hating the person or themselves, or coming on with so much negative emotion that no resolution can be found.

Several years ago, when the Internet first hit, I had a Web site constructed for product sales. I was so excited to get it up and running and remember feeling good about being a part of the new e-commerce. Then, a friend of mine who had been successful in Internet business called me. "Saw your site," he said.

"Yeah? What did you think?" I asked.

"You would have to have a GPS to find a way to buy something. It won't work."

Talk about raining on my happy day. But, he delivered his opinion in a tone that was "neutral." It was negative news, but neutralized by his tone and care. He did not put me down. He just delivered reality. It was helpful, and I fixed the site.

But, what if he had been harsh, arrogant, or demeaning? I could probably not have used his feedback as well. I would possibly have been reeling more from the interaction than from the problem, which is the main point. People of integrated character do not have extreme polarized emotions that make the truth unusable. They have taken the "sting" out of the hard truth so that they can use it to make things better.

And they "neutralize" positive things as well. If there is good news, they do not get so manic that they cannot see reality and the other parts of the picture that are part of the truth too. More about this below in the section on splitting, but it is important to look at the tone of the truth when it comes to you. Is it so harsh or stings so much that you are crushed by it? Or does good news bring on so much elation that you forget that there is a real world to still deal with? Maturity brings truth, care, and reality all together so that no aspect is left out.

## Judgment and Emotional States

In a very real way, we have more than one brain. Or, at least more than one system in our brain. One of them "thinks" emotionally, and subjectively, and the other more logically and with reason and judgment. On a good day, they are partners and work together. It would not be far off to say that they "inform" each other and add to the decision-making of each other. In a balanced character, they are good friends and work a little like a small committee.

But like any other committee, this one is subject to "takeovers" as well as harmony. In a real committee, one member may be more powerful than the others and overtake the process and end up calling all the shots. Our brains can work that way too. If the emotional side becomes overpowering, we can be vulnerable to making some really bad decisions that show poor judgment.

The integrated character, as a pattern, does not do that. He or she, over the long haul, maintains balance between strong emotions and judgment. While he may "feel like" losing it with someone in a rage, thinking things like "I could kill him," he doesn't. He still has access to all of his thinking faculties, and the emotional state that he is in does not "override."

So, one issue is that of the power of emotional states. Now remember, when we discuss character, our definition is not about whether someone is "good" or "bad" in the moral sense. We will discuss morality in the section on transcendence. What we are always talking about is someone's "ability to meet the demands of reality." When a person experiences emotional states so powerful that their thinking ability is diminished or overridden, then the ability to meet what reality is asking them to do at that moment is lessened.

We can all relate to this. Think of a time when you have gotten some really bad news and were just not up to making big decisions at that moment. You might have called in and taken the day off, knowing that you were not going to be a lot of help to anyone until you were able to metabolize what had happened. Or, even on a smaller note, you have a tough interaction with someone right before a meeting, and when you go in, you just aren't "all there." Your mind is overcome with the power of the feelings that the previous encounter had. All of this is normal.

Besides power, the other issue is that the feeling side of things is totally subjective. It "thinks" in global terms, for example. In other words, if something is sad, and it is powerful, the "whole world" looks bad at that moment. Recall your high school friend who found out that she was not getting her braces off in time for prom. Life was over. A subjective emotional state has little access to some of the aspects of thinking that tend to give structure and understanding to the meaning of the emotional event. So, if something fearful happens, or something bad happens, the subjective state becomes "what is" and does not remember that it will be OK, these things take time, help is available, we need to get more facts, we will survive this, business is a cycle and it will turn around, everybody loses sometimes, other projects are working and doing well, other people love you even though this one person is ticked at you, someone somewhere can fix this, it is not the end of the world, etc.

So, put the power of some emotional states together with the subjectivity of emotions themselves, and you can make some awful decisions if you do not have access to your rational, thinking self. In one sense, you can trace a lot of success to this very component of character. In business, there are ups and downs. The winners to a degree are "above" the roller coaster of it all and deal with reality as it is, not as they feel about it. When a deal goes sour, they buckle down and think their way through it. Conversely, they are able to regulate positive emotions as well. When they have a big win in the market, or with a product, they don't immediately "bet the farm" on that same thing. They think through the need for reserves, diversification, investment, profit taking, and other "wise" strategies that were decided upon when cooler heads prevailed. It is the business equivalent of falling in love. They do not have one good weekend, pack up everything, and follow the new lover to Vegas and get married because it was "so good." They know to use both sides of their brain.

From the parent who gets upset with the teacher and instantly yanks her child out of that school, to the CEO who gets cold feet because of some bad numbers and changes strategies without thinking through the implications, the ability to control your thinking when your emotions are enflamed is huge for success. I have seen people literally throw millions of dollars away because their emotional states overcame their good judgment. Because of the strength or the subjectivity of what they were feeling, they just made stupid decisions. The integrated character does not do that.

Why? Strength of resolve? In a sense yes, but in another sense no. It is not as if someone who is overcome by feeling states has a weak mind, or a weak will. It is more a question of what they are walking around with inside that has not yet been metabolized, worked through, understood, expressed, and resolved. Anyone who has had a lot of trauma and not worked through it all yet can be subject to this kind of issue. So, we are all vulnerable to the possibility. It behooves all of us to be working on whatever unresolved pain we are walking around with, lest some issue in "reality" tap into it and overcome our ability to make good decisions.

The other issue may be not that the emotions are just too strong, it may be that the thinking brain needs to be grown some too. As we will see next, it may be subject to "all or nothing" types of thinking, or "catastrophizing," or may just not ever have had enough structured experiences to internalize that help calm the person down in times of intense emotions. In that case, the growth path is to begin to talk those strong feelings through with someone who can help the person to internalize some thought processes to serve as an internal calming agent for the emotional escalation.

No matter what the cause, the wake of people's lives turns out much differently if they are not overcome by their emotional states and retain good judgment no matter what they are feeling.

## Jekyll and Hyde

Everyone knows someone who is referred to as Jekyll and Hyde. That usually means that they are like two totally different people. While that is the extreme, we can all relate somewhat to the concept. The technical term for it is *splitting*. What it means is that some aspect of ourselves is not connecting with another, sometimes its polar opposite.

The most common and familiar form of this is the split between "good" and "bad." It is the tendency for a person to experience themselves, others, or the world as either "all good" or "all bad." It is the hallmark of immature character formation. I say immature, as it is a *normal* developmental stage of thinking and perceiving in which everyone starts out life. If you think about it, you don't meet a lot of infants or small children who are having a "gray" day. It is black or white. They are either happy and smiling, if they are warm, fed, held, and dry. Or, it is rage city. There is not a lot in between. They do not think, "I am a little uncomfortable, but it could be a lot worse. She did feed me a few hours ago, and for that I'm thankful. Hope it is not too long before she comes again." In fact, they don't really "think" at all. They feel and perceive, without much thinking. They experience what we refer to as states, i.e., the state of things being either "good" or "bad." This includes themselves, others, and the world.

This is fine if you are under three years old, and not managing people, or trying to accomplish things, or be a spouse, a parent, or anything else that requires mature thought processes. But if you are, and you see yourself, others, or the world in terms of all good or all bad, then you are going to miss a lot of reality and make some less than wise decisions.

I was in a meeting where a guy was being discussed for inclusion on a project. He had many strengths and could have added a lot to the direction of things that were being considered. He also had some areas of performance that would not have been a good fit. When one of the directors came in and was caught up on what we were discussing, he immediately reacted, "No way! The guy's an idiot! He is just an idiot. There is no way we are bringing him in."

"Wow . . . what was that about?" I remember thinking. Before I asked, the director answered. He went off with a lot of feeling about a project he had worked on where the other guy didn't do things the way the director had wanted. He described it contemptuously, as if the guy were the worst human he had ever come across. It said much more about the director than it did about the man being discussed. I logged it in my mind to be careful when hearing his evaluations. Further, I logged it to be careful to not trust him with too much, as it was clear that if I ever frustrated him and got on his bad side, there was no getting back to the other side, at least easily.

We will talk more about this tendency in the section on embracing the negatives and resolving them, but for now it is important just to see how splitting operates. When people see things in polarities, in either-or or black and white, for example, they miss a lot of reality. In failure or when they make a mistake, they see themselves as "all bad" and get thrown for a loop. Also, if anyone else frustrates them or makes a mistake, they can do the same thing. If a project runs into a problem, it "turns sour."

The mature character, however, does not do that. She sees the world in what psychologists refer to as whole representations. In other words, when she looks at a person, even one who has frustrated her, she sees that person as the "whole" of who they are and not just that mistake. So, she sees someone's strengths as well.

Similarly, when looking at outside realities, the mature character can see the whole picture, without just seeing one side or the other. Watch some of the news shows where a political issue is debated and see the absolute incapability of some people to see the whole picture. They can only see one pole, especially when emotion gets involved. The ability to deal with complexity of all kinds is a hallmark of the mature mind. Children, for example, will immediately tell you that if someone takes something from someone, they did something bad. An adult understands that if a police officer commandeers her car to catch a fleeing murderer, something good has happened.

For mature functioning, we cannot operate well in seeing the world in either-or terms. It is like trying to play tennis with only a forehand and not a backhand. There are a lot of shots you just cannot get to. It is frustrating to work with or to be in a relationship with someone who cannot tolerate "gray" or any degree of complexity that challenges their rigid thinking. Resolving conflict is more than difficult, as resolution usually requires an ability to see and work with the truth from the other side and integrate it into yours, finding a solution that transcends either polarity.

## Seeing It Differently: The Ability to Assimilate and Accommodate

I got into the elevator with the president of a company that I was doing some work with, and he asked me for my business card. The year was around 1993 or 1994, right when the Internet was beginning to gain steam. I handed him my card, which had my new AOL e-mail address on it. He took it and kind of stared at it for a moment.

"Is that an e-mail address on your business card?" he asked, looking somewhat askance at the whole thing.

"Yes," I said.

"Why in the world would you put an e-mail address on a business card?"

"Well, with all I am reading, it looks like the world is going to be doing more and more business using e-mail and the Internet as time goes on. They are saying that it is going to be used even more than faxes and other methods of getting documents and information to people in the normal flow of work," I said, trying to make my case for being an earlier adapter.

He shook his head, rolling his eyes, and said, "Oh, that will *never* happen." Looking at him, you would have thought that he had just talked to the biggest idiot on the planet.

But, I remembered his reaction. Not because he was not informed as to what was going on in the world, but because of his orientation to new information that challenged his view of the world. It was not as if he took in the information that I presented him, thought about it, questioned it, and then disagreed with it. It was as if it did not even get in, period. My information to him was immediately pushed back, like water off a duck's back. Or shot down like one of those little pop-up figures at an arcade. It was immediate and somewhat reflexive. I could sense his rigidity.

This got me interested in his performance. I learned that he had a history (he was about fifty years old) of joining companies at a particular revenue level that had potential, applying good discipline and structure to their operations, and growing them by doing what they were doing better. Then, he would get them to a certain level, around 60 million or so. At that point, they would just flatline and stay the same. There seemed to be a ceiling in his ability to take a company in that industry past a certain level.

As I worked on a few more projects with him, I could see why. He took what was before him and already existed and worked it diligently, squeezing the best out of what was already there. He was highly disciplined and thorough. But, he could not make any shifts or changes in things that required him to see new ways of doing something, or to take in any new information past his way of seeing the world. If something conflicted with the way he understood the world, it was rejected as wrong or not true. Therefore, his chances of making things better were slim. He could only make them more of the same.

This process is called assimilation and accommodation. Which means someone has graduated past childhood levels of information processing and can adapt to reality and make external reality their own. I will repeat that for emphasis: it is the ability to make external reality one's own reality. When you think about it, that is pretty huge. It is a good thing for your view of the world to be the real one. If it is not, you lose a lot of functioning. Think for example if you had to travel from Pittsburgh to Los Angeles and the only map you had was drawn seventy-five years ago. There is a lot of reality that you would not be working with, like a bunch of interstates that did not exist then. Those external realities would not be a part of your map of the world. You have your inside view, and that is that. So, that is the way you operate.

To change, someone first gives you the new information, that new roads exist that you did not know about. If you are open, you take that information in. That is assimilation, the taking in of new information. At least it gets in.

The second step is accommodation, which means that you accommodate the new information into your view of the world, the way you accommodate a new member of your family. You make room for him, or her, and the family has changed. So, with new information the map of the world changes. You accommodate the information and change your view. You now see the world differently, as one that has interstates that can get you there quickly. Not only that, you see the world "accurately." Those roads really do exist.

Immature characters, or nonintegrated characters, ward off new information for a variety of reasons. Sometimes it is arrogance, like a know-it-all character. Sometimes it is pride, like an "I don't want to admit I am wrong" character. Or it could be the anxiety and fear of having to adapt to new realities. To live in a world that is certain, albeit inaccurate, is more secure. To give up false security for reality is for the more mature, and strong of heart.

I followed this man's career, and now he runs a retail chain that is pretty much stuck at the same revenue level, but operating efficiently. It runs way behind its competitors, even in the same locale, and looks right out of the eighties. But, everyone is pretty secure, as long as they don't run out of fax paper, since he doesn't believe in new technology. But, if they do, that's OK, because there is a mule somewhere that can deliver some.

Think of the recent example at Apple. Steve Jobs and crew must have noticed what others did not. The way that music was being used by consumers was about to change dramatically. With digital music so available, and so transferable, there was a new reality to deal with. They assimilated that reality, and then made a huge accommodation. They created an entire new business that has become the very term for listening to your music on a hand held. "Put it on your iPod," people now say, even if you have some other device. Apple made a huge shift because they saw reality before others, or at least they accommodated it into their strategy better than the rest. Now with video, they are continuing to accommodate even further. Can you imagine what they would have lost out on if their character had been closed, and they had said, "Oh, that will never happen" and could not let the new data influence them?

The wake implications for nonintegrated character in this regard are huge. What if your teenager is acting out, and you are bugged and using only discipline to try to address the problem. You take away privileges and ground her. But, she withdraws, and the sullen rebellion gets more sour and worse. You see rebellion as simple, that it should be dealt with strongly, nipped in the bud. And there is huge truth to that.

But, as you are floating along, you find yourself sitting next to a guy on an airplane who tells you that he had the same problem with his fifteen-year-old daughter. And then he says that he read a book that said that sometimes the acting out can be because the child feels cut off from one or both parents, and that he found that his work schedule had caused him to lose touch with his daughter. When he got focused on her and began to try to connect with her and her world more, things changed. He used to see it as a one-dimensional problem of disobedience, but found that other factors were involved, and he had to make some changes in his life and do things differently.

Now, what happens? If you can assimilate that information, take it in, and accommodate it, make some changes in your view of where acting-out behavior comes from, you can transform your family. But, if you are rigid and are not prone to assimilating and accommodating, then chances are you are going to lose your daughter.

The same thing happens in marriage, or a significant relationship, where one's view of the way a relationship is "supposed to be," or "how women (or men) are," is out of touch with what is real. When someone is open to assimilating and accommodating what he or she does not know, things can prosper. If not, he or she can stay stuck or, more often, sour.

A lot in business has to do with this process. The market changes, the customers change, delivery methods change, needs change. In *Good to Great,* Jim Collins tells the story of the difference between Kroger and A & P. One saw that the world was changing and people wanted supermarkets, not grocery stores. So, the company assimilated that data and accommodated. They changed *everything*. And they won, big-time. They exited properties, revamped them, and morphed. But A & P just continued to do things for the way reality used to be. And they lost, big-time. Their map of the world was inaccurate. To understand how far off someone can be in seeing reality and missing opportunity, think of the record executive who, when seeing the new band the Beatles, said that the guitar was going out and no one liked their sound. Talk about rejecting a lot of reality.

If the train companies, it has been said, had seen that they were in the transportation business and not the train business, they might have assimilated the new information that airplanes were here to stay and made the shift. Music companies, for example, have to realize that they are not in the cassette or CD business. They have to assimilate that the world is different and people now want to download their music. As a result, they have to accommodate that reality or they will not be around for long. What if Microsoft had not accommodated to the information that people actually preferred clicking on an icon more than memorizing and typing commands? The world would be on Mac.

Cognitive and emotional flexibility is key for fluid performance and negotiating reality. This requires integrating one's fears, biases, judgments, history, pride, arrogance, paranoia, insecurity, laziness, and a lot of other things that it means to be human. That is what integrated characters do, though. They do the work that it takes to mature, and as a result they are able to "meet the demands of reality" in their personal lives as well as their professional lives. The ones who don't accommodate their view of the world to what the world really is cannot meet a lot of reality's requests of them to perform. And they still send a lot of faxes to their customers who buy cassettes.

There are few things like the ability to say, "Oh, now I see." It ensures that one is getting closer every day to seeing what reality is, in oneself, others, and the world around one. If people can do that, their ability to meet whatever that real world demands of them goes up exponentially. And their wake of relationships and goals met is much, much different from that if they are continuing in their own world.

# CHARACTER DIMENSION THREE

## Getting Results

# 9

# finishing well

think for a moment about your training for whatever work you do. By and large, it consisted of information and experiences about "the work." If you are a doctor, you learned about the diseases and the treatments. You learned a lot about how to diagnose them and what to do to help. If you are in sales, you were trained in acquiring customers, your product line, and closing deals. If you are in a technical field, you were trained how to design it, update it, fix it, or adapt it, among other things. If a CEO or manager, you learned the disciplines involved in running and operating a business. But, no matter what you do, for the most part your training has been about the work itself.

But, as you have gone through the years and worked in your field, you have noticed something. A lot of people know the "what" of the work. They know the facts, the processes, what to do, and even how to do the work itself. They know as much, or more, about it than others. But, they do not produce impressive results. They are not the huge performers. You may even have wondered that about yourself, as well. You know what to do, and you work hard at it, but others for some strange reason seem to do more or better than you. Sometimes you do not understand why, because you may "work hard."

What is the missing ingredient? What could you be doing differently to make it work? Why do the ones who do better do better? Certainly there are various factors to bringing about results, some outside our control. Markets change, economies fluctuate, and other things happen. Sometimes it just seems indecipherable why success comes to one person, project, product, or enterprise and not another.

But, over the long haul, luck and flukes aside, there is a method to the madness. There are "ways" that high producers, those who get results, operate. There are patterns to the ways that they behave, think, and relate that they tend to have in common. And, just like everything else we have seen so far, these have more to do with the ways that they are "glued together" as people than "what they know." It has to do with the character that meets the demands of reality. People who are constructed in a certain way tend to get more results and work in different ways from those who just "work hard."

The sad thing is that we do not think about this when we think about "training" for work. We focus entirely on the "what" of the work, instead of the "who" the person is doing the work. In over twenty years of consulting with leaders and organizations, I have observed that most people know what to do in their field. But, the ones who do well, do the what in a very different way from those who don't, and it has more to do with who they are as people than what they know. All things being equal, character wins.

Yet, how much training have you had in developing the kind of character that will affect the results you get in your job? Who has ever shown you what traits you need to make it big? How many retreats has your company taken you on to work on your "makeup" as a person? How many courses in college or business school instructed you in the ways that you needed to grow as a person in order to make it in business? What were you taught about character?

As we saw in the earlier chapters, most often when talking about character and work we hear about a "work ethic" or "commitment," or things like that. Those are certainly important, for if someone never shows up or quits soon after beginning, then they are not likely to last long. But, the truth is that lots of people work hard and are committed and do not achieve huge results. The reason is often that they do not have the aspects to their makeup that make for real results. It is those that we will examine here. Who do you need to be to make it all work?

## Know Who You Are

My friend began a satellite network and has been very successful. But, before he was as successful as he is now, he had to have an intervention, of sorts. In the beginning when he was starting the company, he did what he naturally did, and he did it well. He envisioned an idea, went around and garnered support for it, got people to join it and invest in it, pushed through the obstacles to get it up and going, and did it. From nothing, to something, and something good. His service added value to his customers and to the viewing public. It was good. But, it was just that, just "good." He was like a lot of people who work hard and get some degree of results. However, that is not what we would call a huge success. It is more like "doing a good job." His desire, and most people's desire, is to do more than just "doing a good job." It is to reach their full potential.

He decided that for that kind of growth he needed more money. To get to a higher level, he was going to have to expand into new markets and new areas of programming and services, and he could not do it at his current capacity. So, his answer was the same as a lot of people's: more cash. "If I had more resources," they think, "then I could do so much more." So, he went looking for the money.

That is when the intervention came. In the looking for more cash, he found more than cash. He found wisdom and had to make a character shift as well. When a group of experienced investors came in and looked at his company, they agreed with him that there was huge growth potential if they added more capacity and expanded into new areas. But, they said something else. They said that they would only put in their millions if he would take something out: *himself.* They wanted him out of day-to-day management and a seasoned operations manager brought in. And they wanted him to focus on exactly what he was good at: creating vision, partners, strategy, alliances, and new services. In other words, do what he was good at and stay out of the kitchen.

What occurred was exactly what experience and research tells us will occur: growth and success. People do well when they do what they do well and stay away from what they do poorly. Is that not common sense? Yes, but when did common sense have much to do with people's business practices? And more to the point, what does this have to do with character?

People who do best in life have a well-defined *identity* on a number of fronts. They are secure in their boundaries, they know what they like and don't like, what they believe in and value, and they love and hate the right things. They are not wishy-washy and what psychologists call identity diffused, wondering who they are or what they are about, or thinking that they are everything. You get a good definition of who they are just from being around them.

Part of that distinct, discrete identity is in knowing what they are good at and what they are not, and they live in their areas of strengths and talents and do not spend much time thinking that they are something they are not. In that way, not only do they work hard, but when they are working, they are working on things that have a chance of succeeding. As we mentioned, Marcus Buckingham and Donald Clifton highlighted how high achievers are the ones who spend their energies in the areas where they are talented, not in their weaknesses (*Now, Discover Your Strengths* [Free Press, 2001]).

But, for this to happen, the person has to have character integration around the areas of strengths, gifts, and talents. First of all, *they have to be in touch with those things.* It is not unusual at all for people to have been defined by others for most of their lives and to be out of touch with who they really are. I recall one doctor I worked with who was a surgeon, but really only because his father and grandfather were surgeons. The family script was already set: he would do what they had done. And he did, for a while. Because he was so smart, he could do it well enough, even though his real gifts were in the arts. But, because his identity was so tied to what his family thought he should be, he did not fully embrace who he really was, until . . .

Over a few years, he found himself in a few nasty malpractice suits because of "mindless" errors. He made mistakes in surgery that had little to do with anything other than not being *fully engaged.* He was there, but he was not there. His heart was not in it. Before long, the hospital that his grandfather had begun agreed, and they decided to move him out. His father was dismayed, as he was not "following in the footsteps" that had been laid out for him. But, he moved to another city and started over.

When he did, he found a new life, one with a very different wake. He got involved in the arts, where he was truly gifted, and it was as if he had found himself for the first time. He was fully there, fully engaged. Full engagement has to do with operating from the center of one's being, and for that to happen, you have to be in touch with who you are and not with "being" someone else.

People who have that kind of character have not succumbed to other people's expectations or definitions of them. They have had the strength to stand up to those pressures and say, "That is not me." As a result, they are internally defined and clear. But usually they did not get there overnight or without conflict and struggle. To find who one truly is usually requires experimenting and risk taking, and if people are afraid of failure, for example, they stay in their comfort zone and never step out and try anything new. That is where character issues get in the way of identity formation. A person who lives life according to his fears is always limited in his identity, as he cannot step out to find out what is really him and what isn't.

This kind of character and identity confidence is a paradox of humility. Upon first glance, the confident "I am good at this" person is not what we think of as the picture of "humble." But, at the same time, because these people are also certain about who they are *not,* and what they are *not* good at, they do not come across as grandiose, just confident. Humility is not self-deprecating, but real and honest. When someone is who he or she really is and does not act as if he or she is *more* than he is, that is not arrogance, but secure identity. Out of that security, competent action flows and results happen.

Because these kinds of people are humble enough to know what they are not good at, they do not think they are something they are not and try to operate in those areas. Therefore, they perform poorly less often. Entrepreneurs who are successful often learn early on that they are poor managers. So, they begin things and then turn them over to people better at operations than themselves and avoid losing the value that they have created. And managers who do not fool themselves into thinking that they are creative visionaries do not step out into nothingness and lose everything. Successful people stick to what they are good at and find ways to make that larger. Usually, that involves surrounding themselves with people who are good at the areas they do not possess. In Collins's words, not only do they get the right people on the bus, but have them sitting in the right seats on the bus.

But, if people are narcissistic, and their image of themselves is to be something "more" or different from what they are, that character flaw is going to do them in. For example, if they idealize the CEO image and think they need to do that to be cool, they may miss the incredible career that they could have had as a good number two. Some people are incredible number twos, and lousy number ones. They could be a star in one role, and a washout in the other. Their character will dictate where they end up. Narcissism, giving in to external pressures, or chasing an ideal image of themselves will take them in the wrong direction. But humility and secure identity will take them in another, leaving a much different wake. I remember a man walking up to me in corporate training and saying, "My career really took off when I finally realized that I was not the type of person to own my own business. I got a good position here and it has been upward ever since. I am so glad I faced that truth about myself." Humble, yet competent and successful.

## Ready, Aim, Fire

Every undertaking has a process with various components. You can break the process down in many ways and stages, but one that I find simple and that really reveals character is the components of **ready, aim, fire**. Results more often come when all of these stages have been added to the process, and none skipped.

Being ready means that someone is prepared, and able. You can

have a great opportunity come along, and if you jump in unprepared, or unable to complete it for whatever reason, you will fail.
One simple way of illustrating this is just in terms of money. If
someone is not ready for a venture by being properly capitalized,
she is going to run short halfway through and go broke. If she is un-
derresourced with people or talent, then the same thing will happen. She jumped before she was ready.

If an individual's character is impulsive, then getting ready or
prepared or up to the undertaking is not usually in the cards. These
people's credo is more like "Fire, Ready, Aim." They jump in before
they or other things are ready, get in over their heads, then crash
and burn. *Their impulsive natures lead them into either half-brained ventures or
good ventures for which they are unprepared.*

Typically, people like this do not have the discipline to do the
things that preparedness calls for: due diligence for a deal, or for
hiring someone, for example. They are so eager, and the waiting
calls for such a delay of gratification, that they impulsively jump in.
And they pay dearly.

Due diligence in any area of life takes a lot of delay of gratification, and patience. For some, that seems boring. They need the "fix"
of the deal. They need the manic excitement of jumping in.

But when you look at the truly successful people over the long
term, they do not make impulsive, rash decisions. They can wait,
plan, look at all the angles. I wish I had kept count over the years of
how many people I have heard say, "I wish I had taken my time with
this deal (or hiring this person, or marrying this person). I found
out a lot of things later that if I had taken the time to learn, I would
not have had to deal with. I would have fixed them first or not gotten into it at all." It is a lesson that experience teaches those whose
character does not dictate it from the beginning.

In describing the different components of what he terms "emotional intelligence" that lead to success, Daniel Goleman, in *Emo-*

*tional Intelligence* (Bantam, 1995), cites the research of psychologist Walter Mischel at Stanford University. He tested the impulse control of children at age four and studied the kind of predictive ability that character trait had for long-term success. It turned out to be a better predictor of their later achievements as students in high school than IQ. That is exactly what we were saying in the early chapters regarding the inability of brains and talents alone to make someone successful. Without character as the vehicle that drives the brains and talents to the contest, we can't get there and win. Goleman puts it this way:

"What Walter Mischel, who did the study, describes with the rather infelicitous phrase 'goal-directed self-imposed delay of gratification' is perhaps the essence of emotional self-regulation: the ability to deny impulse in the service of a goal, whether it be building a business, solving an algebraic equation, or pursuing the Stanley Cup. His finding underscores the role of emotional intelligence as a meta-ability, determining how well or how poorly people are able to use their other mental capacities."

To get ready requires waiting and doing the "nongratifying" work before jumping in. It is the pilot doing the checklist, the surgeon scrubbing down and reading the medical history, the deal-maker doing the market studies and pouring over the financials of the company he wants to buy, the manager doing extensive interviews and reference checks before hiring the "charming" person, the marketing group finding out first if the dogs really do like it, and the "romantic" running a TRW on the person she thinks she wants to marry after a month of dating, or going through divorce recovery therapy before jumping into a rebound relationship.

In the last chapter, I mentioned Rick Warren, the author of *The Purpose Driven Life* and pastor of Saddleback Church, the one with eighty thousand members on its rolls. When he set out for California to begin his mission, he knew his aim would be Saddleback Valley, California. But before jumping, he equipped himself with the facts. As he says to other pastors who want to impact a community, they must get ready:

"If you are serious about having your church make an impact, become an expert on your community. Pastors should know more about their communities than anyone else. As I explained in Chapter 1, before moving to my community I spent three months studying census statistics and demographic studies so I could determine what kinds of people lived in the Saddleback Valley. Before I set foot there I knew how many people lived there, where they worked, how much they earned, their educational level and much more" (*The Purpose Driven Church* [Zondervan, 1995], p. 164).

Another aspect of being ready is readying *oneself.* That has to do with "sharpening the saw," training, doing self-maintenance, etc. In leadership, this translates into getting an organization ready itself before it attempts to do what it desires to do. Sometimes a restructure is needed before entrance into a market is undertaken, for example. But, if a leader does not have the character to wait on that kind of boring stuff that has no immediate return, then he will omit that kind of work. And the organization pays later. Getting oneself or one's organization "ready" may mean training, learning, changing, revamping, restructuring, or a host of other things. But the winners are ready before the game. Long-term high achievers are rarely the type who always wing it. They are prepared.

"Aim" has to do with focus. It has to do with *purposeful, goal-oriented action that knows where the energy and resources are being spent and therefore spent well.* A lot of people spend a lot of energy working, but their character is so scattered that they never focus on particular goals and outcomes and keep on track to get there. A linear path requires the character to say no to impulses and wishes to do other things, to say no to new opportunities that may be good but are not best. Some people's makeup is such that they still think they can have everything, and as a result, they achieve nothing. They are all over the place. If they were to focus, or aim, and direct all of that energy and talent toward specific, particular goals, they would succeed.

Focus often has to do with limits. A person who rejects limits or is in conflict with limits will lack focus. He may reject accepting the limits that time and energy are imposing, thinking that he does not have to live in that reality. He gets sidetracked because he refuses to acknowledge that if you want to do A, you cannot do B. In the end, neither one gets the attention they need.

Picture a little child in a candy store or a toy store. He sees something and says, "I want that one." But before the clerk can get it out of the bin, the child's attention is distracted by another item farther down the aisle, and he has forgotten the first one. "I want that one" is what he says upon seeing the second item and is taken away on a whim. What is interesting is two things. First, he has forgotten the first one. His focus is gone. Second, you never hear him say, "No, I want *that* one instead," when seeing the second one. There is no *instead*. He has not changed his mind as a mature person does and made a different decision, realizing that he has to let go of the first one to have the second. He is just carried away by his wants and lack of focus.

Now, take that character structure into adulthood and you will see a lot people you know and work with. They begin things and get distracted in other directions before following through to completion. Or they do follow through, but they have added so many things that the first one becomes a fraction of the success that it could have been. Details are overlooked, and quality of work and achievement suffer. Coworkers are frustrated and feel let down or not paid attention to. Sometimes clients and deal partners feel the same way. Each person and project becomes the last "forgotten candy."

Reality is that time, energy, and resources are finite. Focus is about directing those in a way in which enough of each is given so that things happen. A focused dropping of continuous water can drill a hole in rock. But much more water in a scattered shower will do nothing. It is ADD applied to life: a lot of activity, but no results.

And the last of the three, fire, means that the person is actually able to pull the trigger. She can, after getting ready and getting focused, go for it. She is not risk-aversive, if the risk makes sense. A lot of preparation has gone into the plunge, so that risk is minimized. That is the difference between an investment and gambling. You cannot really prepare for rolling the dice. It is going to come out the way it is going to come out, and other than researching the odds, that is about all you can do. But an investment risk is jumping in the water after you have found out that it is not poison, toxic, or polluted. Sure, you could still get struck by lightning, but the chances of getting hurt have been lessened compared to if you were jumping in an unknown swamp and had not taught yourself how to swim.

But to finally be able to jump is important. Some people, even after intelligent evaluation of risks, do not like to sow. They are afraid to put the seed in the ground and trust the process. They can't see the seed, and what if it doesn't rain this year? It is just too scary for their character. Again, we get back to that reality. The ability to make a move, make the call, face rejection or loss, is a character issue, and if it is missing, results do not happen. Fear of failure, rejection, disapproval, anxiety, unknown outcomes, loss of security, and other fears keep people from achieving the results that they could, if they were not afraid.

People of integrated character do not think of failure that way. They think that if things do not go well, *that is another reality that they will deal with and overcome.* In a sense, the integrated character never sees failure as an option. These people just see problems to be solved, and they will meet the challenge when it occurs, so "go for it." If, they are ready and have gotten focused on what the goal is. The chute is packed carefully, the training is complete, the landing area is in sight and circled off, so jump out of the plane.

The balance, integration, and order here is the key. Ready, Aim, Fire in concert is a mature person. If the order is off, and someone is Fire, Ready, Aim, or Aim, Fire, Ready, or if the balance is out of whack, Ready, Ready, Ready, Ready, Ready, Aim, Aim, Aim, Aim, Fire, then there is a problem as well. The integrated character, while certainly having areas of strength, has a balance of all as well.

## Willing to Make Hard Calls

I was once working with a parent-toddler group when I heard one of the funniest and yet incredible stories I had ever heard. It may be one of those "you had to be there" events, but I was rolling on the floor with tears in my eyes. The moms were talking about the difficulty they had dealing with people in their children's lives. Many of them began to say how difficult it was to change doctors or schools or other things that involved hard decisions that would upset people. Then Jane made her confession.

"Well, I am embarrassed to tell the group what I did . . . but . . . never mind," she said.

"Come on, you are not getting off now. You have to tell us," the group chimed in.

"OK, but you guys are going to think I am an idiot. But our nanny has not really been doing that great. We have been displeased a lot with a number of things, especially her discipline. She is really nice, and I was just afraid of what would happen to her if I fired her. But, it was just not good for Ashley. And it was affecting my work because all I would do was worry when I was at the office, and then I would not get things done, and yet I had to be there. So I decided I had to do something.

"So, I went home one day to let her go. I went into the backyard and told her that I needed to talk to her, and when we sat down, I just realized I could not do it. I just thought of how it was going to hurt. So, what did I do? I went inside and called my husband and asked him to come home and do it. He could not believe how much of a wuss I was.

"The next day, he came home and talked to her, and I figured it was all done, but I had to leave and did not get home that night until late and did not talk to him. He left the next morning, and then the nanny showed up. I was confused, but didn't want to talk about it, so I avoided her and went to work, thinking he had given her a week or so to get it all finished. I was just glad it was done.

"Later that day, he came over, but another woman was with him. They came in and he introduced her quickly and pointed her to the backyard where our nanny was, and she went out there and began talking to her. I had to find out what was going on, so I asked him who she was and what she was doing there. Then he told me the most embarrassing thing that shows how screwed up we really are. 'That is the lady I hired to fire the nanny,' he said. 'I couldn't do it either.' So, there you go. We are so out to lunch that we had to hire someone to fire our nanny. Help!"

The group was laughing, with her, not at her. All of them could identify with how difficult it is at times to make the hard call. Now think about this . . . what are her or her husband's chances of huge success until they get over the queasiness of making decisions that are going to upset someone? At best, they will limit themselves, trying to keep everyone happy.

To accomplish things, hard decisions are going to have to be made that have adverse effects on people. If you are not in the business of delivering lottery winnings to people, then probably your work is going to involve some hard calls that people are not going to like. And if you are going to deliver results, then the greater those results, and the bigger the position you are in, the harder the calls become. A mother sometimes has to upset someone in her role of guardian and protector of her child. A manager has to make hard calls as the steward of a department or brand. A CEO has to make hard calls as the one responsible for the life and performance of a company and its obligations to its customers and stockholders. And a president may have to even go to war and send men and women into harm's way to protect the country.

Past being mean and uncaring, virtually nothing erodes respect in a person more than his or her inability to make the hard call. In contrast, the ones who can, gain and keep the respect of those they lead. Jack Welch was heralded as one of the greatest CEOs of recent times, and a lot of that came from his ability to make hard calls. Lincoln made the hard call that led to a nation being at war against itself.

"In your hands, my dissatisfied fellow countrymen, and not in mine, is the momentous issue of civil war. The government will not assail you. . . . You have no oath registered in Heaven to destroy the government, *while I shall have the most solemn one to preserve, protect, and defend it*" (Lincoln's first Inaugural Address, italics mine).

In some senses, the degree of responsibility, which really is what success is, that someone rises to rests upon their ability and courage to make the difficult calls. And that is not a brains issue, but a character issue. The fortitude to take the heat, the criticism, the rejection, the backs turning on you and maybe never forgiving you for doing what needs to be done, is the issue. A doctor's decision to amputate a limb, a CEO's decision to close down a division, leave a product line, or restructure a company, or a parent's decision to move the family for what's best, all will have negative fallout. But, the patient, the company, and the family will be better in the end from that ability to meet that particular demand of reality.

## Somehow Finds a Way

When I was twenty-nine, and starting my first real company, I learned a valuable lesson:

> Things never work. When they don't, that is the time
> to make them work. Then, if you do, they work.

I had the dream to begin a psychiatric hospital treatment center in which I would have total control of the treatment strategies, the materials, the milieu, the philosophy, choosing the team, the whole thing. I wanted to construct a place that used the best treatment possible, putting patients first above all else, and build something that would last and become a center for not only treatment but research, training, and community education as well. It was an exciting vision.

I don't have time to tell the whole story, but it went something like this:

I constructed the plan including all of the treatment programs and protocols, and strategic alliances, and got the investors and the management team all signed up. Our plan: find and buy a hospital and then implement the vision. After six months we found our first obstacle: no one would sell. At that time, hospitals were just too profitable, and in California there was a certificate-of-need law that almost insured a monopoly for existing hospitals. So, no hope of buying one. The investors went away, and the management team moved on to another venture in nursing homes. That took the better part of a year. I was back to square one.

But, the vision was strong, and I was young and did not know any better. I thought it could be done, I just had to find a way. I had everything to start a hospital but a hospital. Just one more obstacle. Then, I had a breakthrough. I found a partner from another part of the country who operated several hospital units in the South, Midwest, and East Coast who had relationships with national hospital chains and wanted to move into the West. One of those chains owned a hospital in Long Beach that they wanted to turn around, and they were willing to give us a surgical wing to convert to psychiatry. Finally, a hospital. Also, with the new partner in the mix, the scope of what could be was enlarging, so I brought in a partner as well, Dr. John Townsend.

Now we were in a different world, as we had to operate in an existing medical environment that we did not have control of. And they did not like psychologists, not MDs, running things. So, we recruited the best psychiatrist we could find to be the medical director and got through the politics of it all with much travail. Finally, after so long and so much work, we were ready. We had an opening date, the doctors were lined up, schedules were drawn, marketing money spent, advertising secured, nursing staff hired and trained. It was so exciting. One month from opening and my dream was becoming a reality. Except for one little hurdle that suddenly appeared.

*I read in the morning paper that the company that owned the hospital had entered Chapter 11.* I could not believe it. After all of this, everything ready and in place, we are in a sinking ship that is about to go down. I could not go down with it, but I could not go forward without another hospital.

I did not know what to do, other than pray and hustle. It seemed so hopeless, though, as I had been searching for some time now for a facility that would allow psychologists to do this, and this is the only one I had found in a year and a half. How was I going to find one in a month?

After a thousand phone calls, we got a lead. A little doctor-owned hospital about a half hour away had done some entrepreneurial ventures that were a little out of the box. So, we went to see them. It was comical, when I think of it now. Here we were, a few kids convincing seasoned doctors nearing retirement to give us a wing of their hospital to do what we wanted to do, never having done it before. And, at this point, we had no money to market it, as that was part of the deal from the other group that fell out. But, what's one more obstacle?

I will never forget the meeting where we sold them on the idea, then asked the unthinkable, at least for us. We wanted them to give us another floor of outpatient office space for our clinic rent-free, and furnished. And, uhhmmm . . . cough, cough, we need you to pay production costs and radio-time costs for us to launch a radio show to let people know what we do and to buy all the ads for that. I almost ducked when we got it all out of our mouths.

For some strange reason that I will never understand past what felt like God parting the Red Sea, they said OK. Maybe they were just gladiator fans and wanted to see us get eaten alive, so they provided the arena. But, they said yes. And we opened within the month.

I could continue with more, but will just give one more example of the obstacles. One year later the billing agreement was not working out for us, and we were once again without a hospital. We had to start over. This time we found another national chain who owned one another half hour away, but needed to be brought through the state licensure process for psychiatry. That included construction and a remodel, as well as state inspections and the whole bit. Just to get started again. But, we did it and continued operating.

Within a few years, we were operating in thirty-five cities in four states, and it worked. We continued operating for nine years, and it was one of the most rewarding and exciting periods of my life. From that came the opportunities for so much learning, re-search, training, corporate and organization consulting, publishing,

personal growth, speaking, and media that I would never have had
. . . *if we had given up when we hit the obstacles.*

I do not mean to hold myself out as some model of character, as
I still have a long way to go. But, I can say that if we had not persevered, the many roadblocks we encountered would have stopped a
very successful venture from ever coming to fruition. I have since
learned this lesson over and over and seen it hold true in the lives of
others as well. The ability to keep going when we hit an obstacle,
believe that there is a way to get it done, and keep going until we
find it is one of the most important character abilities that we can
ever develop. It is one of the most important aspects of character
that leads to success.

Perseverance takes courage, stamina, emotional reserves, judgment, creativity, and other aspects of character to do. But, without
it, great things just do not happen. People fold every time they hit a
roadblock. They get discouraged and are controlled from the outside, instead of from the inside.

## Loses Well

I was speaking to parents one time about raising kids with successful character. In the Q and A a woman raised her hand and asked,
"If you could tell parents what the *one thing* is that is most important
to teach their kids about success, what would it be?"

"I would teach them how to lose," I said.

The woman tilted her head, looked at me strangely, and said,
"Why in the world would you want to teach them how to lose?"
After all, we were talking about success.

*"Because they will,"* I said.

She just looked at me and slowly nodded.

Her slow realization seemed to mirror the equally slow learning curve that most of us have about this character trait. After all, no one wants to go through losses to learn how to do it well. Why practice pain so you know how to go through pain? That makes no sense. So, since we want success instead of failure, we do not often focus on losing well, other than to teach people how to be graceful after a sporting event or an election and to congratulate the other side. But that has little effect on future success.

So why learn how to lose well? The reason is twofold. First, as I told her, we will. We all lose. Things will not turn out well and will sometimes be unable to be fixed, even through more perseverance, creativity, and resourcefulness. Sometimes, it is just not going to happen, and in fact, more perseverance can even lead us further down the wrong path, wasting resources, time, and energy. We need to wave the white flag. So, losing is a reality that everyone encounters, and therefore we need to learn how to negotiate it.

But second, and most important, the difference between winners and losers is not that winners never lose. The difference is that winners lose well, and losers lose poorly. As a result, winners lose less in the future and do not lose the same way that they lost last time, because they have learned from the loss and do not repeat the pattern. But losers do not learn from what they did and *tend to carry that loss or pattern forward into the next venture, or relationship, and repeat the same way of losing.* Therefore, they do not become people who lose, as does everyone, but they become people who never win because they do the same things over and over that led to their last loss.

The first aspect of losing well has to do with the ability to let go and just face the reality that you have lost. As Ecclesiastes 3:6 says, "There is a time to search and a time to give up." The Vegas version is "Don't throw good money after bad." Either way you want to say it, the truth is that sometimes it is over, and more effort, attention, or work is wasteful. But, some people, because of character issues, just can't let it go. They can't face the loss and reorganize in a new direction. It is the dead of winter and they are still looking for fruit on the tree. Better to use your energy to get ready for springtime so you can sow seeds that have a chance of growing.

I once watched a company chase the bad idea of their CEO into near bankruptcy. Everyone was telling him that it was away from their core business, their strengths, and what should have been their focus. But, he was *emotionally tied* and invested in the idea, for reasons that had to do with his makeup more than either the mission and purpose of the organization.

His emotional investment kept him from the reality that it was failing and was just never going to work. He overidentified with the idea and was so in love with the glamour of it all, and the tradition of it all in his industry, that he was unable to let it go any more than some people can let go of an unrequited love. And that is exactly what it was, as this project never reciprocated the love. He took money and people from important and profitable operations and markets and invested them in his pet project, and almost took the whole company down. Not until the banks and partnering alliances stepped in and set the limits that he did not possess did it stop.

Integrated characters deal with loss well. First of all, they do not deny it, no matter how much they might love the idea or the endeavor. They can face up to the reality that it is gone. As in losing a loved one, they can grieve. If you have ever seen healthy people go through a loss, you have noticed that they face the pain, then reemerge after the grief and have their hearts available to life again. There is a springtime after the winter of grief. They are not lost in what has been lost and stay there.

On the other hand, you have seen people who cannot lose someone and reemerge. Psychologists call this complicated bereavement. It is the inability to move through loss in the normal stages through resolution. People get stuck in denial, or anger and protest, or sadness, or despair, and cannot move on. This has to do with their makeup, not the nature of the loss itself. Losing is a part of life, and healthy people do it painfully, but successfully. They reinvent and go on.

It is a similar process in both relationships and reaching goals. People's ability to make something work has everything to do with their ability to let go of something that does not work, grieve it, and move on. If something is lost and cannot be fixed, then it is time to wave the white flag and surrender, let it go, and make it something in the past. There is a reason why some people are able to lose and come back, and others stay stuck. They can't surrender and face the feelings and the meaning of some loss, so they hang on to something that is dead. The big idea that successful people always have the character to live out is:

Cut your losses and move on.

The next aspect of losing well is to look back after you let go. After the hope for something to work is relinquished and the defeat is embraced, the *reasons for the loss are examined, understood, and learned from.* If the person does that before moving on to another venture of the same kind, then the loss will not have to be repeated. Again, this is true in both relationships and reaching goals. If someone goes through a divorce, for example, and, to deal with the pain, quickly runs out and gets into another serious relationship, the statistics are clear. The chances of failure go up dramatically the second time around. The reason is that nothing is different. The same patterns that contributed to the first breakup will manifest themselves in the second relationship, and it will likely fail as well. The same thing happens in business. The patterns that contributed to the last loss will contribute to the next one. We tend to fail in the same ways until we change those ways.

But, the winners do not repeat things. They do not blame the broken relationship on the "bad" ex or the last loss on a "bad" market or the "bad" partners or ex-boss or leadership or company. While all those things might have been contributors, they realize that they themselves were a part of the picture as well, and their responses even to bad external conditions could have been different. After all, there *were* companies and relationships that survived those same issues, conditions, or dynamics. So, they ask themselves, what was the difference? What could I have done differently? What did I not see? How do I need to change? What new resources will I need next time? What kind of personal growth do I need to go through for this not to happen again?

In the same way that successful football teams watch the films of their last game and look for the things that led to that loss that they need to change, people who win in life look at their own contribution to failures and losses—and learn. They see the character issues, the communication patterns, the attitudes, behaviors, beliefs, defenses, fears, ignorance, and other issues that helped to make them fail. And they work on those and change them. It is a formal autopsy and postmortem review that proves beneficial. Divorce recovery is a good example. The people who go through a program like that instead of jumping into a new relationship are wise.

In the same way that we metabolize food, we metabolize experience. Experience becomes our character, as we have seen earlier, just as food becomes the cellular makeup of our bodies. You are your experience, in certain ways. It shapes you and forms you, metabolically. You take food in, then break it down into what is usable, and what is not. Your body takes the good part of the experience and keeps that to make new cells, energy, and the like. Then, *what is not usable, it eliminates.* If your metabolic processes are working well, you do this day in and day out. But, if they are not, either you tend not to be able to take what is good from the food, or you fail to eliminate well. Either way, you are getting unhealthy and unable to perform.

In metabolizing experience, the process can break down in the same way. Taking in the good parts of a losing experience means that we learn what we can from the experience and take that forward as new "cells" of our character, meaning wisdom. Also, through persevering and continuing to go forward and reengaging life, we develop strength, patience, hope, optimism, and a host of other important character traits that we will need to make things succeed. But if people have attitude problems in failure or loss, or continue to protest or blame, or even blame themselves, then they do not experience a lot of the things that a loss has to teach us. They just go forward to repeat it again, since they have not changed.

Similarly, if they cannot grieve it and let it go, they do not "eliminate" and are constipated and become toxic. We are designed to be able to grieve things (notice your tear ducts) and move past losses. When we do, we remain healthy. But that only comes through metabolizing the loss, taking what is good forward, and leaving what is useless or toxic behind.

I worked with one company whose CEO had had major successes as well as some big failures over twenty years. In a strategic planning meeting with upper management, we charted the success and failure of the company, looking at its strategic initiatives. *In each case of colossal failure, it had been entered into as a "rebound project" following a loss of a major project loved by the CEO.* When something that he loved had not worked, he immediately came up with a new big idea that he romanticized and entered into, *as a way of avoiding the natural depression and feelings of loss that followed the last one.* Management began to see that their biggest change would be not to enter into new initiatives until they had first figured out what had gone wrong with the last one. But, autopsy had not been a part of the corporate mindset, until the board removed the CEO. At that point, they got a leader who was more interested in not repeating past mistakes than pursing new, "exciting" plans to temporarily keep from being bummed out.

To sit with failure and loss, and understand it, process it, and grieve it before going on, takes depth of character. It takes a well of emotional resources that can fuel the soul and spirit while one is doing that kind of work. The empty person, needing the next manic "fix" of excitement and optimism, cannot wait. She has to jump in. The mature one carries the optimism inside and knows there will be another day, but only after she has fully lived this one. That way, this day won't have to be lived again.

## Losing When You Haven't Lost: Losing 501

To let go of something that isn't working is a sine qua non of healthy people and high performers, as we have seen. But, that is entry level to the field of successful living and achieving. The high performers go a step further. *They let go of things that are working, if they are not the best things.* What that means is that they are able to let go of things that take up time, energy, and resources that may be good, and even profitable, but are keeping them from the best things. The good is the enemy of the best.

In my book *9 Things You Simply Must Do,* I talked about a friend of mine who built a company with annual sales now around $700 million. He began it with a much smaller division of another company, which had many different operations. After buying that small company, less than $25 million in annual sales, the first thing he did was to get rid of 80 percent of the *profitable operations.* They were all making money, but as he looked at them, the real potential growth was in the other 20 percent. He did not want the company spending time, money, and resources on things that were taking him away from where, as he put it, "the real life of the company was."

I have come to see this as one of the hallmarks of both healthy as well as successful people. They can throw things away, put simply. They are not "pack rats" of personal or business activities. Things that are taking away from the future are given away to charity or, if they can't be used by anyone, put in the trash. They are taking up space that can be used for the future. In retail, this is why the good organizations move things out at the end of the year, to make way for what is coming. Keeping all of that old inventory, even though you could probably sell it over time, is not a good idea. They need the shelf space and focus. Shed the skin.

But, others cannot let go of things they deem "good," even if they are not the best. They are dominated by sentimental overinvolvement or attachment to the endeavors, or fears that if they let them go, they might never replace them: "What if I never find another one?" or "What if we can't replace the revenue?" The answer is that you probably won't as long as you are attached to the old things that are keeping you from the new. At some point, a child has to get rid of the tricycle if she wants to ride a two-wheeler. But, throwing the old one away is a little sad and sometimes scary. Winners do not worry about that, but let go of things that are keeping them from what they truly value. Shedding one's skin to make room for the new one is a good practice. You can't have both, and often, underneath the old one is a bright and shiny new one ready for the new season.

## More Than Working Hard

So, there is more to the character aspect of work than a good work ethic. As we have seen, working hard, consistently, with diligence and perseverance, is paramount. But, depending on how someone is put together, it is possible to work hard, be committed, sacrifice, and persevere while at the same time not achieving results. Results are the fruit of other aspects of our makeup as well.

If fears, narcissism, pride, emotional ties, emotional and spiritual emptiness, or other character issues are in the mix, then the work is going to be mixed up with the fruits of those issues, instead of the fruits of labor. The wake will be one where the goals were not reached, the mission and purposes sacrificed to the altar of personal immaturity. That is why success and fruitfulness depend as much upon focusing on the "who" you are as much as the "what" of the work you do. Invest in your character, and it will give you the returns that you are looking for by only investing in the work itself. You can't do the latter without the former.

# V

# CHARACTER DIMENSION FOUR

## Embracing the Negative

# eating problems for breakfast

I was looking forward to the meeting with the big guns of the public company. I was then in the psychiatric-hospital business, and we were about to do our first deal with an entity that large. Up until that point, I had only dealt with small companies, or single hospitals. I remember that as I walked into their headquarters, I was wondering what all goes into making something that big. I just could not imagine how that kind of growth occurred. Surely they started somewhere, I thought, but how they got from there to here was a little incomprehensible. Maybe it was because I was in that mind-set that the experience stuck with me so vividly.

I went in, met the team, and the VP of marketing said, "OK, let's go to the war room and get this done." I did not even know what a "war room" was, but it was the inner sanctum where they did their planning. I did not know exactly what to expect, either, but I was new at this and pretty young, so I was eager to see what a war room was.

I do not to this day have any recollection what that room looked like—how it was designed, decorated, apportioned, or anything about it. All I can remember is that on the far wall was a huge sign that read:

No problems, no profit.

I just stood there for a moment and stared at it, and now, eighteen years later, I still stare at it frequently. It is forever etched in my mind. That's because it answered the question that I walked in with and has been one of the answers to explain the growth and success of so many people I have seen since then. The ones who succeed in life are the ones who realize that life is largely about solving problems. The ones who can get with that find much success, and the ones who can't, don't.

Scott Peck, in *The Road Less Traveled* (Touchstone, 1978), began by saying, "Life is difficult." And then he said, "Once we truly know that life is difficult—once we truly understand and accept it—then life is no longer difficult. Because once it is accepted, the fact that life is difficult no longer matters." It was a psychiatrist's way of saying the same thing that the leadership of that company was saying to its employees who entered that war room: if you orient yourself to the reality that nothing *good* is going to happen if you can't deal with the *bad* things that are going to happen, then you are ready to have something good happen. If you can get with that idea, then you are in the program.

But, if you can't orient yourself to that reality, nothing good is going to happen, because that reality will not go away. It is still the nature of the universe. It will be true that in your business life, personal goals, and relationships, you will encounter problems. Period. If you are not prepared to meet them and resolve them, then they will be the end of your hopes for making anything work, either personally or professionally.

"If Soichiro Honda's orientation had not been towards embracing and resolving problems, we would never have seen the Honda motorcycle or the sweeping influence he had on the automobile industry. He was legendary for tackling problems and obstacles, and resolving them. He even went back to technical school once to figure out why he was having difficulty with pistons. Not allowing obstacles to get in the way, he embraced them and resolved them. That is character."

Orienting oneself to and intellectually understanding that life is about problems is one thing. Being *equipped* to deal with them and resolve them is quite another. This is one reality that requires mature equipment, very complete equipment if done well. It is only the equipment of character that is able to meet the demands of negative realities and transform them into all things profitable. What are the aspects of character that enable a person to "meet the demands of *negative* reality," resolve them, and produce good fruit?

## Does Not Avoid the Elephant in the Living Room

I was at an Easter gathering one time and my friend who is CEO of a company and I were catching up. I asked him how things were going, and he said, "I am about to hit a rough spot. I am leaving for a long trip, and before I go, I have some difficult relational issues this week that I have to *face into*. I need to get them cleared up before I take off, so I have scheduled an entire week of what are going to be difficult conversations. It could get pretty tough."

I was struck by the phrase that he used: *face into*. On another oc-

casion I heard him use the words *lean into*. It spoke volumes, especially to a psychologist who is trained to pick up on the "ontologi-
cal" implications of people's language. What that means is that we
give away a lot about who we are by the way that we speak. Passive
people, for example, tend to talk about events in a way that removes
them as actors, and instead as their being "acted upon," or not a
cause of what has occurred. "I ended up" as opposed to "I chose to."
If we listen to the way people talk, we learn a lot about their "being,"
and how they are "in the world," as the existentialist would put it.
The way my friend talked said a lot about the way that he is "in the
world."

He saw problems as issues to face and lean toward, not away
from. And he *scheduled* the event, as opposed to waiting for it to happen, or worse, actively avoiding it and running *from* it. He wanted to
deal with the issue promptly, actively, and directly. And he wanted
to make sure that he did it before his trip, because he did not want
the problem to linger and cause more damage than it already had, as
well as hang over him while he was gone. He wanted it resolved and
out of his life and company.

What occurred to me is that this is how he lives his entire life.
He does not avoid the problems, personally or in his business. He
has been rewarded in his career for his integrity and values-driven
business and has grown a company based on prompt addressing of
customers' problems and solving their issues in ways that leave
them better off than before the problem occurred. He has also been
chosen by governments to do business in special projects that others were denied because of his reputation as a "fix what is wrong
with integrity" kind of person. So, this one little instance was nothing other than the way he operates. In his wake he has left many
satisfied partners, customers, employees, and others, as well as revenues in the billions. He epitomized "no problems, no profit" in the

way of "face problems and become very profitable," relationally and financially.

The key here for our look at character is twofold: First, integrated character does not avoid negatives, but does the opposite— actively seeks them out to resolve them. Second, integrated character does not see facing negatives only as something painful, but as an opportunity to make things better and get to a good place.

> Profit comes as a result of facing problems, so doing
> it is seen as a *good thing*, not a negative thing.

A rough analogy is going to the dentist. If you have a tooth that is sensitive or you have difficulty using without pain, you can't wait to get that fixed and get back to enjoying being able to eat or sleep through the night. You look forward to having it resolved. So, you want to get to the dentist as soon as possible so normal life can return. Right? Well, that is true *if your past experience with dentists has been good and has led to resolution of pain without a lot of trauma.* You see it as a good thing.

But, and this is a big but, *if your past experience with dentists has been traumatic, and painful, you have a dentist phobia, and you avoid going. So, the avoidance keeps the pain going.* You don't face the problem, so you don't experience the "profit" of getting it fixed. The difference is in facing the demand of reality, and having the character to do so, based on experience.

As a result of the character abilities, successful people face into embracing problems and negative reality. The equipment they carry inside allows them to do this. And part of it is this mind-set and attitude that facing it is going to be a good thing in the end, not a bad thing. But that has everything to do with a person's past experience. I have been amazed at how talented and competent individuals will allow their careers and relationships to be stalled or even destroyed by avoiding the negative realities that make them uncomfortable.

Remember Brad in chapter 2? He was the CEO who was facing a big problem and not dealing with it. Enamored with Rick's numbers, and fearful of losing his performance, he just went into overt denial of how bad it really was. In the end, if you recall, he lost his best people and ultimately his job. This was not from a shortage of brains or talent, but courage to face into this problem. The interesting thing is that when you get into the underlying issues with the person, even though it is a business scenario, it is no different from the wife who won't confront her husband's addiction, or the husband who won't confront the wife's control, or vice versa. Or the dog-food executive who won't embrace the reality that things are not going well and it is because his product is awful. To do that would mean really getting out of the comfort zone and putting one's arms around the problem, in a full embrace.

When Tiger Woods was still an amateur, unproven as a professional, the whole world waited for his entrée. Sponsors stood in line to give him unprecedented amounts of money. Some said Nike was crazy as they forked out $40 million, and Titleist another $20 million. Sure, he was an amazing amateur, but the PGA is a different world, and he had just not proven himself. But, everyone waited to see if he was going to live up to the expectations. Not since Nicklaus had we seen anything like this.

Golf is measured in the majors, and Tiger's first Masters as a professional was watched by the whole world. What happened? He won. Not played well, mind you. Not beat the cut or was respectable, but won. And not only did he win, but he won by twelve strokes. Unprecedented. They were right! He is in another world. We have never seen anything like this. The whole world felt what

Bobby Jones had said about Nicklaus: "He plays a game with which I am not familiar."

Now, think about this. You have just won the first Masters you compete in as a pro. You set a record for how big your victory is. You have more endorsements from everyone than you can ever deal with. You are on the top of the golf and sport world, being named PGA's Player of the Year and Associated Press's Male Athlete of the Year. What does he do?

*He decides that he has some problems with his game that need to be addressed if he is ever going to reach his goal of being the greatest player in history over the long haul.* So, he goes to work on his game, making some huge changes that are difficult to make, enlisting a teacher along the way to reconstruct or reengineer his swing. If you are not a golfer, there is something to understand about this. When a golfer does something like that, it is not instant improvement. It is not like "Oh, I think I will do it this way and things will get better. I will beat everyone by twenty shots tomorrow, not just twelve." In fact, it is the opposite. Things get worse before they get better. It is like remodeling a house. You basically can't live in it while the remodel is going on. But, your eye is on the future. It will be better in the end.

So, things got worse. He had what was described as an "off year." He was in the remodel. But, what happened after that shows the truth of what we are saying, "no problems, no profit." He emerged from having the character to "embrace the problems" and tied the PGA post–World War II record of consecutive wins and then goes on to win all four majors, in a row. He has continued on since then to break all expectations and will continue in the future. Why? Talent? Certainly. But there is a lot of talent in the world. My view is that it is also *character. His "ability to meet the demands of reality" is what is breaking records.* He met the demand of fixing the problems in his swing, *faced into it,* even if it meant great pain, bad headlines, losses, critical people, and the like. He was not afraid of going to the dentist and getting it right. Today, he is enjoying the fruit of not only his golf swing, but his character.

The masses enjoy the "comfort zone." They do whatever is most comfortable, even if it is not going to get them to "profit," whatever that is. But the winners see putting their arms around the problem as their way to the promised land, and their character will allow them to do no less. It is a good thing, and you virtually can't keep them away from embracing the negative realities that they need to address. What you hear is "I can't go skiing that day. I have to go to the dentist." Or from Tiger, "I might not be able to win this year. I have to re-create my swing so that I can be the best in history."

To do this requires an absence of internal and interpersonal fears that facing negatives can bring about. If my friend above were too afraid that facing into those confrontations would bring him rejection, or someone would no longer like him because of what he had to say, then he would avoid the conflict. If Tiger were afraid of the bad press or people thinking he was just a flash in the pan, then he would have protected his lead and status instead of ripping it apart. But they were not. They had the internal equipment to desire the outcome and weather the process. "The only way out is through."

One of the surprising things about working with adults who grew up in homes with an alcoholic or abusive parent who truly was the "bad guy" is the set of feelings that they find they have for the other parent, the loving one. Even though the good one was the one who gave them the love and affirmation that they needed, they often have to work through deep feelings of disappointment and betrayal at that parent's avoidance of dealing with the other parent. They struggle with why the good parent never did anything and then often suffer with their own patterns of allowing negative realities to persist long after they should, as that was what was modeled for them. Avoiding the elephant in the living room not only allows the problems to continue, but erodes trust in the one who does and in the nature of love itself.

And this occurs not only in the personal context. The scenario that I described with Brad and Rick is common. The person in charge of a team or an organization avoids dealing clearly and decisively with an obviously hurtful person and loses the confidence of the other people in the team. The leaders who are respected are the ones who can be depended on to deal with things directly and competently. Recently I consulted with a company that was in turmoil for three years, lost several key people, and was not reaching many of its objectives because of the CEO's avoidance of dealing with the president's dysfunction. Finally, as in the case of Brad, the board had to step in. They intervened with the CEO and made him deal with the problem.

What occurred is a lesson for all. Within a few months the entire organization turned around because the problem person had been removed. He had been causing division, a lack of morale, discouragement, and a pervasive negativity, and when he was gone, all of that went with him. The climate changed. You could feel the difference in the energy, as the team clicked and good things began to happen. The lesson is that when problems are truly addressed, they are addressed. The pain can end, and it surprises people who have grown accustomed to putting up with it that things can actually work. And another part of the lesson is just how quickly that can happen. The avoidance takes years sometimes, but after things are decisively addressed, within weeks and months normalcy returns. Even in Tiger's case, in the whole of a career, an "off year" is nothing.

Recoverability

I worked on a project one time with a person who had been highly
acclaimed in corporate circles and was well-known for his accomplishments in marketing around the world. Many organizations
were trying to recruit him for his expertise, and I was excited at the
opportunity to work with him. I was sure that we were going to be
successful in our venture.

The first aspect of it took the better part of a year to put together and would culminate in a launch date that had great expectations. He had assembled several strategic partners and a lot was
riding on its success. Because of his reputation, I was certain that it
was going to do well.

The launch date came with everyone eager for the results. It was
going to be huge, or so we thought. The day after, when the results
were in, he called me. "How did it go?" I asked.

"Well," he said, "I just lost more money in one day than anytime
in my whole business career."

My jaw dropped and my heart sank. I could not believe it. How
could this be? He was the genius that assured success. This could
not have happened. But, then, I instantly wondered about him.
How was he taking this? How was he doing with moving to a new
project and completely failing because of being outside of his areas
of experience? What was I going to do with a failed venture and a
wounded leader?

"So, as I am going over all of this," he said, "there are some patterns emerging in it, and I think some things to learn. It looks like
what we thought we would get from this particular sector got inter-
fered with by the release of some other products, and I think if
we . . ." He was into the problem and had his arms around it, sleeves
rolled up, and was about the business of understanding it and fixing
it. I could see how he had created literally billions of dollars of busi-

ness in his past ventures. One of the big reasons: *he had the ability to recover quickly.*

What psychologists refer to as recoverability is the process by which people regain functioning after a negative emotional event. When something bad happens, are they knocked off their horse, unable to get back up? Or, do they bounce back quickly, suited up and ready for the next blow?

Integrated characters are able to recover motivation, hope, judgment, clear thinking, drive, proactivity, and the other faculties needed to move something forward after something bad happens. The negative news or event does not sideline them for too long. It is not that they are in denial, as we talked about earlier, and avoid the problem or doing the postmortem. It is the opposite, that they have the resources to face into it quickly but without the kinds of emotional, cognitive, and behavioral responses that hamper or make impossible meeting the demands of reality.

Contrast my friend with another guy I will call Michael. Michael thrived on the positive, and things going well. If something succeeded, he was energized and ready to conquer the world. He loved success and came to life with affirmation. But, in this particular season, the market had hit a downturn, and his division hit a downturn. When the numbers started coming in, he started going down. His people were looking for him to lead, to figure it out, to come up with ways of going through this and making it work. Michael was going in the other direction.

As the bad news was coming, he was folding. He began to feel like a loser and questioned his abilities. He lost his confidence, his drive, and his judgment got fuzzy. He started to go into protective mode, when more decisive action was called for. He began to withdraw from the rest of the team and had a down mood, and the people that reported to him began to go to other managers for the input they needed. He was kind of MIA.

His boss was tuned in enough to get him some help. Michael had come from a critical and harsh family environment that he had internalized. He overcame and warded off harsh criticism as a youngster by performing. He was gifted and did well in school and sports, and if he could always get it right, he felt that would keep the abusive anger away. When he would make a mistake, however, he would get mean put-downs and reprimands that were now the monstrous critical voices in his head. As a child, he would retreat into himself and withdraw into seclusion and away from the storm. But he did not have much of a way of getting out of the black hole and self-loathing that the critical onslaughts had left him in. He recalled times of feeling lost and just "out of it," as he put it.

But this experience had never been "integrated" and worked through. So, it just sat there as a part of his makeup that would not emerge until something bad enough, such as the market downturn, happened. When it did, it would make him feel as he had as a child, except this time the voices that put him down and caused him to fold and go into the black hole were inside his head. As we said earlier, what was once outside becomes inside. His experience had become character. The failure, the voices, the withdrawal, the deflation, the negative thinking, and the *inability to recover* had all become part of who he was.

The good news was that he had some new experiences that also became part of him, and the patterns of nonrecoverability changed. He grew in his character. Through new supportive experiences, he developed the ability to recover and "get with it" when negative things happen. If "no problems, no profit" is true, then the ability to recover from them when they show up is huge if the profit is going to happen. That takes character, and character comes from experience. His "slow to recover" character came from old experiences, and his new one from new experiences.

The marital research of John Gottman shows that one of the

predictors of a relationship's ability to last and be fulfilling is the couple's ability to recover from disconnection, conflict, or a problem. His term is *repair* (John M. Gottman, Ph.D., and Nan Silver, *The Seven Principles for Making Marriage Work* [Three Rivers Press, 1999]). If they can do that, they are more likely to make it.

## Separate from Results

One of the abilities that makes someone able to lean into the negatives, face them, and recover is to be separate from the problem or the negative outcomes. Secure identity is about who a person is, not what he does or what his results are. When someone's identity is tied to his outcomes, he or she doesn't exist in a certain way. They are what happens. So, if things are going well, they are well. But if things don't go well, and the outcomes are bad, they are not well at all.

When athletes, for example, hit a slump, one of the ways that performance coaches get them out of it is to help them get separate from their results. Just get in the box and swing, don't worry about where the ball goes. "Decatastrophize" the outcome. It doesn't matter where the ball goes, get back into the experience. A catastrophe is defined as something that causes damage or suffering. For someone to experience damage of the self, or the self's ability to deliver, as a result of a bad outcome is a huge problem.

> Outcomes are separate from the person,
> and the people who perform have a stable sense of
> self no matter what happens.

High achievers do not derive their sense of who they are, or how they feel, from the outcomes of their performance. Certainly, doing well feels good and contributes to good feelings, but that is different from one's feelings about oneself. The results are the results, and the self is the self. That way, achievers improve performance when it is not what it should be by focusing on what they need to do differently and the changes that they need to make. The problem becomes the focus instead of "me." "I need to do A or B," instead of "I am a loser." In the second scenario, A or B never gets addressed because the person is down for the count.

One of the key distinctive elements of an intact character is "differentiation." It denotes the degree to which a person is who he or she is apart from others and from all things external. The identity is intact, so they do not need external performance, approval, image, symbols, riches, organizations or affiliations, and the like to know who they are or to regulate how they feel. In dealing with negatives, this is key, as it allows a person to deal with the problem, or the result, without becoming a part of the problem or being infected by the issue. We saw above how it relates to performance results, in an athlete or a businessperson. It holds true in interpersonal relationships as well.

For people to deal with negative interpersonal realities, they have to be separate from the other person's feelings toward them, or the other person's feelings in general. For example, if they have to have others like them, or not be upset with them, then solving problems becomes virtually impossible. The nature of conflict means that people sometimes have negative feelings toward each other. The one who is separate from the other person's feelings can understand and empathize, without getting off track because of those feelings or becoming what the other person feels she or he is. Also, these people are less apt to feel hurt, damaged, or incapacitated by how someone feels toward them when facing an issue. A good parent, for example, has to discipline a child even when the child hates them for it and looks up and says, "I don't like you!" A leader has to remain separate from how people feel when he is con-

fronting them about performance, or an issue. A dealmaker has to
stay separate from external pressure in negotiations or conflict. To
perform, separateness is everything. Without it, the person's steer-
ing wheel is virtually in the car in the other lane. She is just along for
the ride, not in control of where she is going.

## Ownership

"I did everything according to what the attorneys said. I went right
along with our policy. How can you say that I made a mistake? I followed the book on how to do a layoff," Jim protested when the
president of the company called him on the carpet for a disaster
that he had created in his retail chain. Jim was VP of Human Resources and had engineered a "layoff" as he put it, but the real mo-
tive was to get rid of some store managers, more than a corporate
restructuring. He moved some regional lines around so that those
management positions were no longer needed, but in reality what
he wanted to do was fire some people. Instead, he took the easy way
out. He was afraid of firing them, and besides that, he had not done
the proper discipline along the way to be able to fire them. The
documentation of efforts to remedy their work did not exist. So, he
took the "layoff" approach.

The result was chaos. People began calling from all over the
country, worried about the status of the business. Suppliers were
concerned, threatening to hold back orders fearing that the company would not be able to pay. Morale was shot and the president
found himself in a big mess. And Jim had pulled the trigger that
began it, so he was accountable.

But, Jim was not taking responsibility for the results. From his
perspective, he had done everything "right." He had "followed the
policy and done what the attorneys had said to do." He had done
nothing wrong. But, if that were true, how come now everything

was "wrong" in the wake? What I said to the president was that his VP was not acting like a leader, but only a "worker."

"What do you mean?" he asked.

"Well, workers do a job. They do what they are told, and that is all they are responsible for, in their mind-set. If the desired result does not happen, that is not their problem because they did what they were told. And, at the 'worker' level, they are right. They are not held accountable for results, but for what they do, i.e., whether or not they follow instructions and implement what management tells them to do," I explained.

"But here, this guy *is* management. He is the leadership of the entire way that HR functions. He cannot expect to be held accountable for only doing what a lawyer tells him to do. He must be held accountable for the *results* that his decisions bring about. It was his strategy that created a big mess, and he is not taking ownership for the results of what he did. He just wants to be seen as 'good' and doesn't care about the results.

*"Leaders take ownership of the results and do not try to excuse those or blame someone else for them."*

I encouraged the president to focus on that issue with his leadership if he was ever going to be able to lead. Leaders and, more than that, all successful people do not worry about just making some authority happy. They worry about the results. A quarterback who says, "Well, I can't be bothered by the fact that we lost the game. I really did what I was told," puts a ceiling on his performance and leadership ability. Sounds more like the thinking of the water boy than the quarterback, who is the field general.

It is not enough for the integrated character to be seen as "having followed orders" if the ship sinks or the company is not profitable or his or her child is flunking out of school. Integrated characters want good fruit. They want things to work, and they take ownership of the results as well as their own performance. On the surface, this may seem to contradict what we saw earlier, about being separate from results, but it doesn't. You can remain separate in terms of what the results mean about you and whether you over-identify with them and see yourself as a loser and go into a black hole, while at the same time taking ownership of them and seeing yourself as the one who is going to deal with them or do something different to bring about a different result.

Certainly, there is a boundary. You do not have control of the universe, and at times you do all you can do or, even better, all that could be done, and still a result does not happen. We cannot control other people, or world markets. We can influence them, but not control them. At some point you have to let it go and move on. A lot of parents have concluded this when they have done all they can with a wayward child. At times leaders have to do this with employees or partners too. There is a limit to the ownership of results.

But what I am referring to is the other extreme where people excuse practically every result in their life and blame something outside themselves for what happens. They do not see themselves as contributors to the result, and when they do that, something terrible happens: you can virtually count on it not getting better.

Blame is the parking brake for improvement.

It is in human nature for us to blame and externalize. Children do this all the time. Watch young children who are just learning the nature of right and wrong. When you confront them, they say, "Susie hit me first." Or, "He started it." In effect, what I did was not an issue, 'cause it was really someone else who caused the result.

Successful people care very, very little about "fault." They do not worry about things "being their fault." Fault to them does not have the most important implications, as it does for immature characters. What has the most important implications for mature characters is solving the problem. If it means that they need to do something differently, that the way they did it was part of the problem, to them that is *good* news, not bad. They *love* knowing that. It gives them control of making it better.

Successful people do not blame the outside world for their lack of success in any given venture or relationship. They put their arms around the results and ask themselves, "OK, given this market, or given the cards I have been dealt, or given who this person is, what can I do to make it work?" They see themselves as actors and not those who are acted upon or whose script is written by someone else with a plotline that is going to take them to a crummy ending that they have no control over.

## The Underlying Sickness

So, why would someone do this? Why would they choose to be "performance crippled," instead of being empowered? A few things make up the underlying sickness to blame. The first is the worst sickness of all: the preservation of the "good self." It is the character component of narcissism, the search for the "ideal self," or the wish to see oneself as "all good" or flawless or perfect. It is one of the sickest traits that we can have.

What causes it? One thing is that people may have a lot of shame underlying their wish to be perceived as "good." To cover up their feelings about themselves, they try to perform well and be seen as awesome, wonderful, ideal, and to get a lot of accolades to make them feel good as opposed to their underlying bad feelings about themselves. They thrive on praise and being admired as a medicine to the underlying vulnerability in their souls.

Perhaps they were put down as children, abused, made to be the container of all the badness in the world by a "blamey" parent. They have a "bad self" picture from long ago that they are trying to stay away from by never making a mistake, or being seen as making a mistake. The problem is that they have sought the wrong path to deal with that issue. Their way to overcome shame and the "bad self" is to perform well. But that never works. *There will never be enough accolades to overcome bad feelings about the self.* If there were, why are some of the biggest stars and most worshiped models and performers drug addicts and self-conscious people who still feel "not good enough"? There are just not enough trophies to cure narcissism.

The cure is always to find acceptance and love in one's weakness and failure, and therefore discover that you are not what you do, but who you are. When we are loved for who we are, not for what we do, then we have a character based on being and not doing. That is where the contrast between "human being" and "human doing" comes from. When people are accepted in their failures and find that their imperfect selves are lovable, they are free to own their imperfections and improve. That is why correction that is done lovingly leads to healthier people than shame-based or critical, angry correction. The focus is on the behavior and not the person.

But if people have sought achieving the "ideal self" as the cure, then they are set up for a lifetime of excuses, blame, and nonperformance as they try to be good, instead of effective.

So, to have an integrated, strong character, integrate the "bad self" and the shame with the rest of who you are by talking about those parts of you with people who accept you, instead of trying to hide and overcome them by being perfect or ideal. Then, you will be free to reach your potential.

Another reason people try to preserve the good self is that to acknowledge responsibility for results makes someone responsible for results. That sounds like a truism, but think about the implications. If I take ownership for the failure to get the results, instead of trying to appear faultless, then I am saying that I am in control of making things work, and that might scare me. It means that I have to get off my duff and make it work. To real performers, that is music to their ears. To people who are afraid of failure or hard work or floundering or any host of other things, it is not music at all. It is a thunderstorm and they run for cover. Excuses sound much better than taking responsibility and going through the pain and brain damage that it takes to succeed.

In fact, the word indolent, which we often use to describe those who are lazy, actually means to avoid pain. Excuses and blame, and trying to appear never at fault, are actually some of the biggest ways of being lazy that exist. One who blames and one who gives excuses is often too lazy or afraid to do the work to overcome whatever taking responsibility would entail. That work is painful. So, one of the best pieces of advice we can ever receive is to give up being perfect or ideal and, instead, embrace ownership of the results, go through the pain to improve, and enjoy the benefits. The "good self" is not worth hanging on to, because it won't produce real results. Let it die and a competent self emerge. "Being right" can never compete with "doing well."

Larry Bossidy, former chairman and CEO of Honeywell International, says this in the book *Execution: The Discipline of Getting Things Done* (Crown Business, 2002):

"In his book *Jack: Straight from the Gut,* Jack Welch freely admits he made many hiring mistakes in his early years. He made a lot of decisions from instinct. But when he was wrong, he'd say, 'It's my fault.' He'd ask himself why he was wrong, he'd listen to other people, he'd get more data, and he'd figure it out. And he just kept getting better and better. He also recognized that it's not useful to beat other people up when they make mistakes. To the contrary that's the time to coach, encourage them, and help them regain their confidence" (p. 83).

## Confronts Productively

One of the most important aspects of character in life, without question, is one's ability to confront. It is true that you get what you tolerate. If the nature of reality is that there are always problems, if you do not confront them and instead tolerate them, then problems are what you will have. I have never met or observed a person with a truly whole, successful wake who did not confront well.

This gets us to one of the best aspects of the need for integration in our view of character integrity. Nonconfronters leave a lot of success on the table. Problems overcome them and stop them, for their political tendency for "people pleasing" can only get them so far. We have seen some examples of that earlier in the book. To do well, and to treat people well, we must confront the problems we have with them. And not only do nonconfronters leave a lot of success on the table, they also leave a lot of messes in their wake. Those who are affected by their lack of confrontation, and messes that they allowed, are deeply disappointed in them. Confrontation adds structure to teams, projects, relationships, and life. Structure adds security, and in security people thrive. Without the security that confrontation provides, people and relationships languish. Both intimacy and performance get sick and die. The wake is not good.

But, the absence of confrontation is only one piece of the problem. The other piece is confrontation that is not done *well*. A lot of people confront easily, even too easily, and yet do it in a manner that is more destructive than helpful. The combative or angry or critical, demeaning confronter does not solve problems. He or she usually drives problems more deeply into hiding by creating an atmosphere of fear rather than resolution.

That is why I say that this is one of the areas where character integration is so important. If you fail to confront, you will lose. But, if you confront poorly, you will also lose. So, you must confront, but confront well. That means that the truth-telling side of your character must be integrated with the loving and caring side of your character. When you show up to deal with a problem, you must bring both of them together. Confront the problem, but in a way that preserves the relationship and the person. If you err on either side, the wake will be affected.

We hear a lot of ways of communicating this truth. In parenting, you hear the phrase *love and limits.* That means to be caring and be firm. In theology, we hear *grace and truth,* which means to be "for the person" and have standards. In psychology, we hear *authenticity and love,* which means to be real and caring. However you look at it, the important thing is to say what needs to be said, and to say it in a way that shows that you care about the person.

The best prescription for leaders that I have ever heard on how to do this came from a friend of mine who leads a company. I think it applies to all of life, not just leadership. He says, "I try to go *hard on the issue* and *soft on the person.*" That means that both his truth telling and his care for the connection came together at once. Here you can see the importance of integration, as this one concept brings together three of our character components at once: connection, orientation toward truth, and embracing and resolving negatives. That is why I say that integrity is always about integration as much as it is about honesty. *Honesty without love is not integrity.*

But this requires a character that has neutralized the truth, as we mentioned earlier. If he or she is still running around with a lot of anger inside that has never been integrated and metabolized, then confrontation is going to be toxic, "beating people up." Love and healing must first have taken place inside people's souls, or they might be in danger of treating others not in the way they themselves want to be treated, but in the way that they *have been treated.* They repeat the abuse that they have been subject to in their own experience.

Another aspect of confronting well is that integrated people care about the results of the confrontation, not just about making themselves feel good. So, they ask themselves before the confrontation, "What do I want to have happen as a result of this confrontation?" If they are impulsive and don't do that, then they might just care about releasing anger, or forcing someone to do things differently, or getting revenge and making someone feel bad and themselves feel better. But, if they are mindfully integrated, then what they do is desire an integrated outcome. They think, "I want to solve the problem, make the relationship stronger, help the person develop, and empower their development." So, they confront in a way that is going to bring about that wake.

They also tend to stay connected in two ways. After the confrontation is over, they check in to see how it is before they leave. "So, what are you hearing me say?" They want to make sure that it was clear and also that the connection is good. The other way is that they follow up and see how it is going and see confrontation and problem solving as process, not an event.

Confrontation does not have to be adversarial. It merely means that we are going to "face this issue together instead of putting our heads in the sand and ignoring it." I like the phrase "to turn your face toward" as the meaning of *confront*. It does not mean a military destruction of the other side, but a coming together of two people facing some problem and finding a solution that brings it all together. Poor confronters turn things adversarial too easily and quickly. It is experienced as me versus you, or us versus them, as opposed to this way:

You and I versus the problem.

In that scenario, we are a team against what is wrong, and coming together to fix it. That keeps the problem, the person, the relationship, and the result all in mind in an integrated fashion.

## Lets the Bad Stuff Go

We talked earlier about the ability to "metabolize" failure and losses, in the section on getting results. Nowhere is this more important than in facing not only a loss that is unfixable, but also in a problem that is being fixed. Some people cannot let it go. The vernacular is *get over it*. What that means is that when there is an issue with someone, or a problem that is dealt with and solved, then let it go. Otherwise, you have not solved it, but are carrying it on.

In all sorts of relationships, we see people's wakes being affected by the inability to let it go. If you are going to solve problems in your personal relationships or your business ones, then you have to be able to let things go. I do not mean do not face them, especially if they are ongoing. What I mean is that after they have been addressed and resolved, then let it go in terms of the negative, punitive emotion of it all. Grieve it and, dare we say, *forgive*. People thrive when they have faced an issue, made it right, and the other person can forgive them and move on. *Forgive* means to "cancel a debt." In other words, the person does not owe us anymore. No more wallowing, guilt, shame, reminders, or other things that get in the way of the future. If something has not been fixed or trust regained, that is one thing. But if it is fixed, put it behind you.

If parents can confront and forgive their children, their children learn to solve their problems and move on. If children can deal with things and forgive their parents, they can get healthy. If bosses can forgive mistakes when the mistakes have been owned and faced, then employees can become learners and look forward to the future. But, if we can't cancel the debt and are always sending reminders for some sort of collection, then the problem never really ends. We take it forward. We continue to punish. The people in your life will thrive to the degree that you become a forgiver who is also not afraid to face the problem. Together, that kind of integration fixes things *and* has a future. Forgiving does not mean not facing a problem. It means facing it and then letting it go.

I had dinner recently with a publisher who had come from a family gathering. He said the entire atmosphere was affected by one adult sibling who still wants another sibling to pay for misdeeds of the past. The publisher's mantra over and over was "Just get over it. Let it go!" Until then, future gatherings will be past gatherings, where the misdeeds of the past are gathered together and reviewed, becoming the misdeeds of the present.

But, character integration and wholeness are paramount here as well. People who have not ever really faced their own misdeeds, owned their own mistakes toward others, and received forgiveness and made amends rarely have forgiveness toward others. They still think they are morally superior and lord their superiority over the ones who fail them in some real or imagined way. But, if they have been honest about their own failures and been accepted for those, then they are more humble and able to forgive other imperfect people like themselves.

Confront well, and when people own it and the problem is resolved, let it go. Do not carry it forward, thereby keeping old injuries alive. The future is to be gained, not lost all over again.

## The Best Way to Solve a Problem

Confronting and solving problems is a hallmark of the successful character. But, integrated characters have an equally important function regarding problems as well. In fact, it is the best way to solve a problem:

The best way to solve a problem
is not to have it to begin with.

Integrated characters have a great immune system against getting into bad situations. They sense them early on, and if something smells wrong, or not good enough, they just say no. They do not agree to things that do not fit their criteria, their values, their purposes, or that have too many negatives or the types of negatives that they do not want to deal with. In the section on getting results we talked about the due diligence required before jumping into something, and being ready. This is the other side of that quality: after the due diligence is done, and something is found lacking, one has the character ability to say, "No!"

I have a friend who once gave me some sage advice. He said that he finally got to a point in his life where he doesn't do anything that involves the "cringe factor." He said that he will not go forward in any deal or work with any person having a cringe factor. I did not know what that meant, so I asked him.

"That is the big gulp you would have to take to go forward," he explained. "My rule is this: anytime I have to cringe or take a big gulp to agree to do anything substantial with anyone, whether to hire him, work with him, or anything significant, I don't do it. I won't go forward as long as the cringe factor is there. Period."

Instantaneously I remembered times I had ignored the cringe factor. There were so many situations that I could recall where I had gone forward ignoring problem areas about a person or a deal, but took the big gulp only to have the big throw-up later. I had to learn that lesson the hard way, as most "optimists" do. We can get ourselves into messes that could have been avoided if we had paid attention to the writing on the wall and not taken the step where there was a cringe.

This is like the immune system for the character. It is about "boundaries." It is like your skin. Your entire being is designed not to allow toxins into your system, body, or otherwise. Your skin keeps bad things out, unless a cut allows infection in. Your immune system keeps germs out by immediately dealing with them and saying, in effect, "no deal." The germ is not allowed to become part of the body, but is destroyed and eliminated. And your character has to have the same functions as well, serving as the immune system for the things you agree to do or not do.

But, again, this requires integration. To say no means that we have to be strong enough to disappoint some people, and also to give up some things that we might want because they have too many negatives that go along with them. People who have become immune to pain, for example, sometimes take on problematic deals and suffer the consequences because they do not have the integrated character to pay attention to their gut, which says, "I don't want that!" They have been so numb for so long that they just sign up for more pain and then suffer the consequences. It is as if they have learned to believe that pain is just part of their lot and they don't even much notice it until it is too late.

Other people deny the negative just because they want what is there so much and cannot delay gratification until the right deal or situation comes along. In business you often see managers hiring people just because they are in a hurry to fill the position, and they know that the person is not really what they want. But, to go through the hassle to continue interviewing is too much and they want to get it done. They ignore their gut, and then they have someone that they ultimately wish they didn't. People do the same thing when they get engaged, make partnerships, or even buy houses or do deals. They just don't listen to that little voice that says, "Don't." Here is a list of things that the voice might tell us if we are integrated enough to listen:

- This doesn't feel quite right.
- I really don't feel comfortable doing this or agreeing to this.
- This is not what I really want.
- I don't like what I am agreeing to, or part of me doesn't.
- This violates an important value.
- I am going to resent this later.
- I am going to resent this for a long time.
- I resent this now.
- I wish this were not happening.
- This feels the same as the last time.

(adapted from *9 Things You Simply Must Do,*
Cloud, Integrity Publishers 2004)

Integration says that our character will not allow one part of us to do something that another part of us is not cool with. If some desire violates your values, for example, it is not an integrated move, and the mature person will say no, even if that means loss. But, the good thing is that it means loss of something else that is more important to lose: the problems that going forward would have brought you. Have the courage to say no when it is not right.


## No Pain, No Gain

To face negative things is hard. Otherwise, everyone would do it. To change is hard work, otherwise everyone would grow. I said that the winners freely go to the dentist and get the gains. They want the pain to go away. But, something else is true about them too: they are willing to go through the pain that it takes to get there. They do not see pain as something to be avoided, but the necessary price to pay for what they want.

Character that is mature knows a basic reality and has made it a part of itself: there is no such thing as a free lunch, and whatever has value is going to require hurt in order to possess. Try to name one thing in life that is of value that you do not have to suffer something in order to have. There is nothing. Even the best things in life that are free, as we say, such as love, have big price tags in order to possess. Self-denial, sacrifice, giving, delay of gratification, repentance, forgiveness, swallowing pride and ego, are all among the price tags of making love work. But, in the end, it is always worth it.

Success is the same way. Tiger could have ridden his laurels after that first Masters victory and $100 million or so to spend. What a joy ride for someone who is barely not a teenager and still eating at McDonald's. But, to be the best in history was going to require not the comfort of sitting on easy street, but the pain of change. The pain of facing what was wrong and going through it. That is character integration.

Fixing a marriage, a company, one's own performance, an addiction or depression, a failure, a relationship, and even a physical injury are all possible and done successfully every day by people of character. But, they have oriented themselves to a basic reality that there is no gain without pain. It is hard to fix a marriage, or a business. There is no easy street and no shortcut. In the end, the shortcut is always the longest route, and people of character know this and it has become a part of their makeup. It is the way they think and the way they are.

It begins with the child who is required to do his homework before going out to play, or to eat her vegetables before dessert, or to forgive or apologize to his brother before being allowed to resume the game. But the lesson that is learned is that there are only two ways in life, and the person of character has it hardwired to only go one way:

hard, easy versus easy, hard.

Those are our only two options. We can do the hard work of facing a problem and making the necessary changes to resolve it, and then we will enjoy the easy road of having things right. But the hard comes first and must be endured.

Or, we can take the easy route first and avoid fixing a problem. Then, as sure as the sun will come up tomorrow, the hard life will follow. And it will last a lot longer and will be a lot harder than if we had chosen the hard way first.

People of character, when facing a negative, embrace it. They do the hard work first. They do the hard work before going on the vacation. Then, as a result of doing the hard stuff first, embracing the negative and dealing with it, either in themselves or someone else, they are ready for things to be easy for a long time.

# VI

# CHARACTER DIMENSION FIVE

## Oriented Toward Increase

# getting better all the time

have a friend who has had one of the most interesting business careers. He was a financial guy and went to work for one of the big record labels right out of Harvard Business School. A quick study, he rose through the ranks to become the financial architect of one of the famous labels. It would seem that the success might have made him settle in a comfortable spot early in life. He could just have ridden it for a while, or even an entire career.

What happened was the opposite. As he describes it, a tiring of the "egos" in the business, as well as a "curiosity" to learn and do something different, motivated him to take a step that most highly successful MBAs at that age would not consider. Leave the financial security, esteemed position, and power that he had earned and start over as a neophyte in another industry. Now at first, you might think, well, that's not true. He didn't really have to start over, for he could enter an industry with a good position as a CFO. But that is not what he did. He did not enter as a financial guy, but a learner and a beginner. Desiring more flexibility and to be on his own, and having the curiosity to learn a new business, he entered the real estate world with the goal of becoming a principal in real estate holdings, despite that he knew nothing.

Since he had a young family, a mortgage, and the enemy of all new directions—high overhead—he "pared it down." Wanting to be free from pressure, he sold his big fancy car, moved the family, got an old desk, a file cabinet, and knocked on some doors to find a corner of an office he could rent. He found one at a car-leasing operation that gave him a corner for $50 a month. A big downward swoop from the glitzy corner suites in New York and Hollywood. But, he was curious.

He read, he took courses, he talked to people and learned the business slowly. He began by buying a small piece of property and learned the next step. He got a broker's license. Eventually, he built a big portfolio of industrial space in California. Not a bad way to spend some of those years, if you know California real estate. Once again, he had it made.

Knowing him since the early eighties, I mostly watched his business success and attributed it to his being very, very smart. I did not connect it at that time to what was the real reason: *a drive to grow into "more" than he was at any given moment.* His term for that is what he calls the "curiosity" for "what is around the corner." I should have put it together, because in that span of time, I saw numerous totally "nonbusiness" expressions of the same character trait: the desire to grow, learn, master things, morph, discover, and become more than he was.

In that same period, I saw him enter the world of personal growth, go to weekly therapy, join a 12-step community, and meet regularly with others who were into personal growth as well. At forty, he did something painful. He took up golf as an adult with the goal of becoming a reasonably low handicapper. He was up every morning for a few years in the beginning, hitting balls and taking lessons a couple of times a week. I was there, and in the beginning it was really ugly. The kind of ugly that accomplished people often find too frustrating to go through. But, he persevered. Recently, twenty-five years later he spent a week in Scotland playing the courses that had made the game, and was good enough to enjoy it.

I saw him study and pursue other hobbies with the same curiosity, and he also become a serious cyclist, traveling the world and riding some of the best trails and courses available. He worked hard to learn and develop the skills first, training diligently. The drive, the curiosity, and the desire to grow in these areas was the constant as it was in his business life. He did the same in his spiritual growth as well, pursuing his faith and development there with the same passion for understanding and learning. He read, went to lectures, and kept seeking input.

I never put all of this together as being more than about a business acumen until I was on the phone with him sometime in the midnineties. This was about *character*. On this particular day, it was more than clear.

"So, Terry, what are you up to?" I asked.

"Liquidating," he said.

"Liquidating?"

"Henry, let me tell you something. We are experiencing a once-in-a-century phenomenon. This is like the invention of electricity, air travel, or the telephone. This Internet thing is huge, so I have gone into the learning mode and am getting rid of property right and left so I can focus."

"Learning mode?"

He went on to tell me how he had been spending the better part of the last two years just "learning" about the Internet. He studied

Web businesses, models, technology, and all of it, trying to find out as much as he could with a desire to enter the business. For a long time, he just surfed the Web, looking at how others were doing it. Eventually, he founded an off-site e-commerce monitoring company. That is when it hit me.

He cannot not grow.

He was literally unable not to develop and create what I call increase. It is about "more," but in a different way from greedy people. We will talk about that later in this section, but that was not him. The "more" is about becoming more of who he was as a person, in life, in business, and in his relationships. It was the curiosity and drive to develop into more ability, more knowledge, more completeness, and ultimately, more experience.

Since that time, he has learned another field, back in real estate, and is in the business of rezoning and adding value to properties and cities. As he does that, the investments grow immensely in value, and he either holds them or resells them to developers. This was not something that he invented, but it was something that was new for him. As he went around the corner, pushed by his character, he found great invigoration, mission, passion, and profit.

## The Drive to Grow

People with this character trait leave a wake of making things bigger and better over time. There are some differences in this trait from the previous one about solving problems. When people solve problems, that certainly makes things better. They get better, their organizations get better, their relationships get better. Things improve. But, it is only the improvement of what already exists. If you have a broken arm or an infection and you get it treated, it will definitely work better. You can use it again. But, it will only do what it was already capable of, just now without the hindrance that the problem was causing. It will work better, for sure. But, it will not be stronger or able to do more than before you broke it. It will just be repaired.

In life, some people are good problem solvers, but are not growers. They clean up all the messes that they encounter in themselves and others and, as a result, are pretty clean. They run clean businesses, have clean relationships. Things work, but they don't become *more* than they are. They are good *maintainers,* as opposed to *growers.* In business, for example, there is a great need for problem solving, as we saw, and for people who can fix broken operations. And that can add to the numbers, for sure. But they are not the ones you turn to for a business to grow. That takes a different set of gifts. It gets confusing too, because good operations can add to profits and it will look as if the business is growing, as the numbers are getting better. But, that increase is really about getting all the benefit of what already exists, not building more.

In fact, some of the very processes are the same, as we shall see. It takes effort to grow, and the ability to sustain pain, as we saw, is involved in solving problems. There is grief involved too, as you have to let go of some things to move to the next level. Sometimes the lines get a little blurry between the two constructs, as it is difficult to have one without the other.

Also, getting over a problem sometimes means developing new skills or ways to do something. So, in some ways, problem solving and growth are not 100 percent discrete constructs when they are working well. But, that is also what we have been seeing all along, that mature character is integrated. It is pretty tough to solve problems without also connecting to others and being oriented toward the truth.

> The more we get into this thing called character,
> the more we see that integration and wholeness is
> paramount. It all goes together, and when we are
> stuck in one, it will certainly affect the other.

Integrity itself as a construct is really about the integrated functioning of all aspects of character. They are interdependent, and it is difficult to have one really working without the others.

But, as integrated as they are, there is still a difference in the creation of new capacities and new skills and new areas of fruitfulness. For to meet the total demands of reality, we must be *growing* and always *increasing* our abilities, skills, and capacities, in every area of life. If a toddler just maintained a two-year-old level of development and never increased those capacities, she would miss out on a lot of life. Thus she would miss out on the life that she could have had. To find all of that life, she has to have a "drive to grow." There has to be a force inside that literally drives her to want and find "more."

Integrated characters have this drive inside. It is as natural to them as breathing. Everything they put their hearts and minds to is infused with this drive, to make it better and to make it grow. Their relationships grow, their businesses and careers grow, and their personhood grows. The groups and departments that they belong to grow. They can't help it. It is a drive.

## The Normal Path—Use Creates Growth

If something is alive, it is doing two things, simultaneously. It is growing, and dying. Depending on where it is in its life cycle, one of these processes is probably more dominant, or at least more visible, than the other. You can see the growth changes as an infant progresses quickly in the first few years. The changes in capacity are amazing, physically, emotionally, psychologically, and intellectually. The brain goes through incredible changes. So, the last thing that you notice is that this same child is also getting older and moving toward death.

But, what we also know is that the relationship between those two processes are greatly affected by several factors. One of them is use. The more we use something, the more it is growing and increasing in capacity, and either reversing the death process or at least slowing it down. If an infant is connected with and loved, it thrives in all categories. If it is not loved and bonded with, it suffers "failure to thrive" syndrome, or "marasmus," and can even die. The brain does not develop, the emotional life does not develop, and even the body does not develop because of a lack of love. *The lack of use ushers in death.*

Think of this just in terms of your own muscles. If you use them, they stay healthy and get stronger. Just look at a tennis pro's dominant arm and compare it to the other one. You can readily see how use helps. We simply get better at things that we do. Even the brain works this way. We used to think that you were born with a certain number of brain cells, and you'd better be careful with them, 'cause that is all you get! Now we know that the brain can grow, and with use it can develop even in old age. Literally, use creates life. The old saying "use it or lose it" is true, and now even the science that supports it is making its way into the mainstream. *USA Today* reported on August 17, 2005:

"It's more than just a clever idea. Animal studies and rapidly growing human evidence suggest that adults might be able to delay or prevent severe cognitive decline, says Molly Wagster, who directs research on normal brain aging at the National Institute on

Aging. 'There are no guarantees yet, but it's really looking like some of these things could work.' "

The article then listed several activities that may have this kind of force against "losing it," such as various sorts of mental stimulation, higher education, leisure activities, exercise, and healthy foods. It says:

"The evidence that mentally challenging lives boost brainpower comes from large, worldwide samples of people who have been followed over time. Scientists compare those who maintain good mental function with those who don't. Very few controlled clinical trials have been done, so conclusive evidence on preventing dementia does not exist.

" 'However, animal research, some newer types of brain scans, and human autopsy findings tend to support the population findings,' Wagster says.

" 'What we have is fairly compelling and worth paying attention to now,' says neurologist David Bennett of Rush University Medical Center in Chicago. 'Don't wait till you're eighty.' "

So, the first principle of growth is this: *what is put to use, grows.* But unlike a plant that is placed in the soil to grow by someone else, people are very different, and this is where character becomes everything:

> People do not get put to use by others.
> They have to invest themselves.

People have a choice to invest themselves in growth, or not. It is possible for them to bury their talents (symbolizing many different aspects of themselves) and not put them to use, and then lose them in the end. And that is exactly why this topic, oriented toward growth, lands in a book on character. Growth is something that someone has to engage in *willingly.* It cannot be imposed on someone, and it can also be resisted. So, again, it has to do with the makeup of the person, the character. Let's look at what growers and nongrowers do and don't do, as well as have and don't have.

## The Drive

Things that are alive naturally have a curiosity for increasing experience, skills, knowledge, and other things of life. If you look at children, this is one of the things that stands out the most. They are always looking for the next experience, what is "around the corner." In fact, the big problem in parenting is not to get them motivated, but to discipline and limit their natural motivation in a helpful direction and manner.

Learning how to buy and sell real estate and learning the Internet, stepping out to start a company, is doing what children do, looking for more. My friend is normal, in that sense. The problem is that *normal is not common.* What is more common is people who have had their hunger and passion diminished or injured in some way. They have an "anorexia of life." If you have seen people with the medical condition of anorexia, you know what happens. They have no appetite and have begun to wither, severely. In the same way that our physical appetite drives us to food, unless we are anorectic, our growth appetite should drive us to desiring new experience. As I said, my friend could not, not grow. That is normal, but unfortunately, not always so common.

Other people and organizations do not experience that drive and have gone into a dull state of "maintaining." They are just continuing to be the way they are, day after day. They relate to their spouses, kids, coworkers, and friends the same way, never wanting to grow into relating differently, or more deeply. They go about their careers the same way, doing what they have always done, following the conveyer belt of doing only what is required of them.

Their personal lives are the same way. They dull themselves with only mindless television or reading, or social interaction that never goes below the surface of well-traveled topics, or old patterns. You could almost peer into their lives in the same activity year after year and see no difference. The reasons are manifold. But, they all fall into a few categories. There are ways in which their desire to grow has been injured or stifled. There are ways in which they have not had the ingredients that are necessary for growth. And there are ways that they have not been pushed to have to grow. All of these have incredible implications for our own character and growth in the areas where they apply.

## Buried, Hurt, or Stifled Hunger for Growth

I was recently at the Getty Museum in Los Angeles. People travel from all over the world to see the exhibits, which are amazing. But I never really made it to enjoying them. I was too awestruck by the museum itself. Sitting on top of a crest overlooking the city, it is a breathtaking grouping of buildings that seamlessly takes you from being outside the world of art to being a part of it, beginning with the structures themselves. I was fixated on them, wondering, "Where did something like this come from?" And then, I remembered. It came from the invisible world of an architect, Richard Meier. This astounding creation, visible to my eyes, came from the invisible *character* of a person.

I have never met him, but I can tell you what probably happened. Many years ago, as a young child, he picked up a block or a pen or maybe a brush. He stacked the block on another one, and a shape appeared. Or, he drew a line and noticed a shape. When he did, something came alive inside that did not happen when he played with a soccer ball. His invisible talent found its way to the outside world. And somewhere, someone encouraged that ability and afforded him some experiences to build upon it. Someone en-couraged him and sent him on his way, where mentors and teachers picked up on his talent and built more into him, as well as the char-acter to be disciplined enough to bring it all to fruition. His natural hunger to grow and develop was watered and itself grew. After a few decades, his talent was living in the kind of character that hun-gered for more and created it. In the end, we all get to enjoy its fruitfulness. His wake.

But, there is another museum that we will never see. It lives in the unrealized talent of another would-be architect, Joel. Joel picked up his first block and had a similar "coming alive" experi-ence. But, when he did, someone criticized it harshly and he never tried it again. His family was not supportive of his desire to grow and increase his artistic ability and instead put it down. So, he gave it up, and his invisible talent never did find expression in the visible, outside world, like a museum. He now lives a stable but nonpas-sionate life that never changes much.

> The invisible world of character is where
> the visible world always originates.

You can see how one person's hunger can be stimulated and channeled, and thereby last a lifetime, and another's be injured and lost. Joel basically had growth "anorexia." Joel's drive had been in-jured and stifled. We could look at him and think he is kind of a drifter, not motivated, and while that is true, it misses the point.

The point is that character is about experience, and while he may be drifting, he is not without hunger, any more than an anorec-tic patient is without a natural need for food. But, his *experience has become his character, his makeup.* Here is what happens.

Deep within, when he has a fantasy of doing something or a dream, or just a thought, "wouldn't it be nice," or "that's interesting," that desire doesn't make it far. It is instantly squelched, put down, criticized, and killed off by the critical voice of his early experience, which is now part of his own makeup. It is now he who keeps himself imprisoned. We do not hear that, for the most part. We just see the wake of his stuck life, not alive with new, stretching experiences.

The ability to thrive, relish change, and overcome the gravitational pull of negativism comes from the character of the person, as does the resistance to change, failure to thrive, and the negativism itself. And all of that usually comes from the internalized experiences and fears that people like Joel have gone through and are now a part of themselves.

For someone's character to grow, it has to be free from internal attack. Growth requires taking steps into unchartered territory. For people to integrate new capacities or internalize new skills from the outside, they have to try new things. But if every time they think of trying new things, they get a negative message from inside, then that aspect of themselves remains unintegrated. Growth is stifled when there is internal attack and fear. Compare that to a little kid who knows no fear other than the actual consequence of falling down. *Falling down never stopped children from developing. But getting yelled at, criticized, and put down can stop them for life.*

And past the fear of trying things that they are aware of, there is the problem of losing altogether the drive and hunger to grow. They have become zombies because the internal putdowns have driven into psychic exile their belief that they can do more. They no longer even feel the desire. So, life is a flat line.

The developmental path for this is well documented. It goes in a sequence that begins with desire and growth. If that desire is met with good results, then it is internalized as a next step or skill, and also as the belief that trying itself helps. But, if it is not met with some good outcome or met with a negative outcome, then the next natural response is protest. This is the crying baby who is not picked up, or the employee who is not being heard by a manager, or the spouse who is not getting her needs met. If the protest brings about nothing good, then the person goes into a state of loss, or depression.

This is not what you think of as clinical depression. This is the depression of not having a hope or desire answered by the outside world. It is a state of loss and sadness. People cannot stay there long, just hoping that things will get better when they are not, so they enter into further despair or hopelessness about the issue. When that becomes too much to bear, he or she goes into what is called detachment. Detachment means that the person separates from the wish, desire, or hunger itself and no longer feels anything. As Pink Floyd sang, "I have become . . . comfortably numb." People have lost the ability to want, desire, or believe that it can happen.

Think of how you have seen this in married couples. They long for something to change for so long, and protest the way things are, but get no answer and finally give up hope and don't care anymore. Or the management team that wants things to be different, but is not listened to, and the life finally goes out of the culture of the organization. It is a common process. However, when it becomes part of a person's character, and character detachment sets in, then something really bad happens:

The belief that growth can happen no longer exists.

And where there is no belief or hope for growth to be real, it is no longer attempted. People, or organizations, enter into a state of sameness, and as we have seen, that is really when things are no longer alive. Death is taking over, not growth. It is imperative for you to challenge and overcome the experiences you have had which stifle your drive to grow. If you do that, your abilities can find the outside world.

## Good and Bad Hunger for More

As we have said, the hunger for more is a healthy sign of character. It means the appetite is alive and well. For a company or a person to want more sales, more victories, more territory, is a sign of good things. Or for a person to want more skills or abilities or performance is a sign of life. For a relationship, to desire more intimacy and more experience of each other is a sign of growth. But, the appetite for more can be healthy or unhealthy. Some cravings are nourishing and make one more alive, and others only lead to more cravings and no growth.

All hunger and passion is like that. It can be an integrated aspect of the character that serves all of the person, or it can be disintegrated and keep the person further away from becoming whole. Sex, for example, can be a hunger that serves love, intimacy, connectedness, personal growth, bonding, and a lot of other aspects of being a person. If it is motivated by good drives and hungers, and integrated to all of those things, then it creates growth in a relationship and in a person.

But, if it is motivated by power, for example, or anger or the nonrelational, disconnected lust of a sex addict, then it does not integrate the person or serve his or her relational life or personal fulfillment well. It separates sex from the heart and soul, and the body has a life of its own that cannot find enough. You hear people say that there were just not enough one-night stands to ever fulfill them, but always the need for more.

The character who truly produces increase is one who is creating from an outgrowth of real passion and investment in things that he or she cares about from the heart. The drive to get "more" connected to their life drive, and grounded in aspects of who they are that are real. It is not just a means to be someone people are not. It is the opposite. It is an expression of who they are and whom they are becoming. It is real, and because of that, it has life, force, and is sustainable.

## Gambling, and Taking Risks

Whenever growth is discussed, the importance of taking risks is mentioned. In fact, when people talk about success, the ability to take risks is one of the things that separates the real winners from the also-rans. The winners got out of their comfort zones and took the risks, while the rest of the pack lagged behind and never really got anywhere. That is true. But the way that a lot of people think about it leaves a lot of room for misunderstanding.

*Risk means that you do something that has the possibility of a bad outcome, and that you embrace that possibility and are OK with it.* It is voluntary exposure to danger of some sort. Financial risk means that you invest your money in some way in which it is not certain that all will be good, but there is also the possibility for a greater reward than if you had done something more secure. All it means is that you are exposed. It does not mean that you are an idiot, or that there is a great chance that things will go badly. That is more like gambling than risk.

Successful characters take "risks" in other people's minds, not really so much in their own. Other people look at them and see them investing, or beginning a business, or undertaking some venture, or going out on their own, and think of that as taking a lot of risk. What it really means is that they have put themselves in the position of responsibility. If there is not a good outcome, it will rest on their shoulders. Risk taking is merely taking a move away from structured security where someone else has to worry about the results.

But, is it really risky? No. It usually is not. It is usually very, very calculated. I would not term most of what successful people with venture mind-sets do as risky. I would think of it more as expressing themselves in the ways that they have *already grown and learned, but in a new way or arena.* The good ones learn something and grow to a point where what they are doing can no longer contain all that they have become. So, they just step out and take the next step. They have grown and are ready to take a further step to express the amount of ability that they have developed, and that step creates even more. Stepping out is not a risk. It is an expression of who someone has become, even if he or she is not sure of the outcome.

Growth is like that. People work on themselves, and then they express what they are learning in a further step. When they do that, they become more. It is merely a natural outgrowth of what already is. When a toddler takes her first steps, it is not as dangerous as if she had tried it earlier. It is an expression of the strength that has been gained already, and although the result is unclear, and she might fall down, she is ready to take the step. You can call it risky, but it is really something she is ready to do. Then, as a result of taking that risk, new growth happens.

When my friend quit the entertainment business and stepped out on his own, many of his colleagues considered that a risk. It was, in that he did not know the outcome. But, he was certainly *ready* to take that step. He had done hundreds of deals, knew a lot about business, negotiating, putting money into ventures, capitalization, and other issues like that. He just did not know anything about real estate. He could learn that. But he was expressing the growth that he had accumulated in the previous years and stepping out in a natural progression.

Gambling would be someone who had never done a deal of any kind, or few, and bet the farm and the family's security on somehow hitting it big. That is not what successful people do. They grow as a course of things, then break out of the skins that are holding them back. They do not attempt things that they have no reason to believe they can do, if there is a lot at stake. They attempt things they have never done when they are in the learning mode, but not the investing mode.

Even in the area of relationships we see this same thing to be true. People of integrated character step out and take risks, in that they will be vulnerable and open themselves up to people. But, they do that after they have developed the relationship skills to handle whatever happens. They have the support network to be with them if there is a bad outcome in that relationship, for example. They have grown to the point of taking that next step.

Risk taking is an important dynamic to growth. It means that someone is putting himself in a position of exposure, where he can be hurt. But, that is really just a synonym for being alive. It is risky to drive down the freeway, in that definition. But, if you are going to function, you have to do it. You have to get out there to get somewhere.

People who grow are not afraid of getting out there. But they are not stupid, and they risk in increments. They start small, master that, and move to the next step. As they do, they have grown.

To do that requires that their character has the necessary resources to withstand the possible negative outcome. If it doesn't, the risk was not an integrated risk. It was a wish, not an investment. If someone cannot withstand the negative outcome, then it was not the kind of character investment that leads to growth.

People, for example, who have gone through a divorce and done the growth work by taking the beginning risk of opening up to a recovery group, telling their story, and revealing their pain have grown to the point where they are strong enough to take the risk to begin dating again. Because of their growth from taking those small risks, they are ready to risk the rejection of a dating relationship not working out. They can handle it. It is not a gamble. But people who are divorced and devastated and risk everything quickly in a new relationship are not growing, but foolish. They might not be able to withstand the outcome well. It may do them in.

So, growth requires risk. To grow, you must take the step to the next level past where you are comfortable. But risk that creates growth is the kind that is a natural expression of what someone has already become, not some foolish leap into oblivion. That is a roll of the dice and more akin to a gamble than a risk.

## The Necessary Ingredients

So what does it take to create growth, and what do these "characters" do to make that happen? There are a lot of ways to talk about it, but one of the best ways comes from physics. Whether you are growing a company or a person, you are going to find that growth happens in the same way that it happens in the physical world.

A law in physics, called the second law of thermodynamics, says that entropy, or chaos (the opposite of growth . . . a winding-down process), increases over time. You can readily see this in life, and we have already talked about it. Anything left to its own is naturally dying, getting more disorganized, rusting, etc. Even the universe itself is subject to that process.

But, and this is a big but, the law only applies to "closed systems." In other words, if a system has no way of connecting to things outside itself, then it is getting worse, not better. On the other hand, if a system is "open," and it has two things that it is connected to, then it can grow into a more ordered, or higher order, state of being. What are they?

The first is *energy*. There has to be an input of energy from the outside for something to become "more." It needs fuel. The second is a *template* of some sort. In other words, there has to be an organizing force or principle that shapes the direction of growth. Energy and a template, or force and direction. If you have those two things, you can grow.

Translated into people, what this means is that a person first of all needs to be open. If they think they know it all or do not expose themselves to new experiences and sources of growth, then you are going to get disintegration, not growth. Ask yourself if you are a "closed system." Do you only talk to people who believe as you do? Only engage in your already proven abilities? Do you only take input from old sources? If so, nothing new is coming in. Or, as we said in the section on assimilation and accommodation, is anything able to get in at all?

When someone is open, there is the possibility for an energy infusion. For someone to grow, there has to be a connection to outside sources of energy. Who is pushing you to grow? Who is supporting you to grow? Who is pushing you past the level at which you already are? Where is the encouragement coming from?

> The number one reason for lack of growth
> in people's lives, I have observed,
> is the absence of joining forces outside
> themselves who push them to grow.

Instead, they keep telling themselves that they will somehow, by willpower or commitment, make themselves grow. That never works.

But if they enlist a coach, join a group, get a counselor, a community of growth, or some outside push, then the growth begins to happen. It is the coach pushing us to greater heights, the sales manager motivating you to something you can't do, the Weight Watchers group motivating you to try a new course. On the other hand, if it is all self-motivation, then decay, decline, and dying take over, especially when we hit the stuck places where more is required that we don't have. But, if there is fuel from the outside, we are pushed further than we are able.

Second, we need the structure of the template. This is like the lattice for a plant. It shapes the energy in a particular direction. It is the structure and path of the growth. A training program in a company, for example, shapes the direction of growth. A curriculum for a school shapes the direction of growth for a student. A set of principles that guide a couple to a better relationship shapes their growth toward intimacy. If you are going to grow in some area, you need to have a direction or a path that is going to guide that to a form. Otherwise, you are just shooting off energy that is not going to come together in any sort of discernible fruit. It will be lost. But with a template, it will become something, whatever that template defines it to be.

## Submission to the Structures

Given all of that, the characters who grow submit themselves to experiences of both outside energy sources and templates of information and structure that mold the direction of their growth. The number one indicator that I have found that reveals a person's character is oriented toward growth is the spending of two concrete resources: *time* and *money*. You can always get a picture of people's (or even a company's) drive to grow by looking at their calendar and their checkbook. If they are driven to grow, then they spend these two valuable commodities in becoming "more."

I just returned from an international leadership summit in which the leaders discussed their personal orientations toward growth. One global leader said that about ten years ago, he was near burnout and collapse, as his organization had exploded in size. But, he himself was dying. So, with input from his board, he made a huge investment of both time and money. He decided that every summer he would take six weeks away to study, refresh, get input into his soul, and re-create. He put the number two person in charge with orders to not call him "unless the whole thing were burning down."

The character components of this were substantial. First, there was the courage to leave it all to develop himself. What if it blows up? His answer was that if it did, it was not worth it to begin with, as it was killing him, and second, it would be important for the people underneath him to be put into those crisis decision-making situations if they were ever going to grow also. That is another of the characteristics of people oriented toward growth: they want others to grow as well as themselves. He was not afraid of the consequences of what would happen when he invested what he needed to invest in himself.

Second, he said something profound: "I have never made a decision for my own growth where I did not end up with someone upset about it. When you invest in yourself, there will always be people who get mad at you. I have just learned to live with that reality and will not let it stop me." That takes courage as well.

Third, he spent the money. He invested a substantial amount in this program and has now for fifteen years. To do that requires not spending it on things that would have brought an immediate, visible return. But, in the ensuing years, the organization that he has built has continued to grow even more. Nongrowth characters would not have thought that was possible. They would have thought that they had to be there grinding the crank, instead of investing in themselves. As a result, they would not have exponential but linear growth. He made the character call.

If you look at the growers' checkbooks and calendars, you see them spending time and money on set structures in their lives. These things are in the calendar and do not get moved, unless the "whole thing is burning down." In successful people's lives, there is no time when they "have time" to do things that are future-oriented. The present is always too busy. *Therefore, they do not wait until they have the time. They make the time, first.* Then they do what the present calls for. Here are some examples of what their calendars and checkbooks reveal:

- Personal coaching
- Personal therapy
- A support group of other executives, parents, or people in personal or spiritual growth
- Training experiences
- Continuing education past what is required
- Retreats
- Accountability relationships
- Summits of other leaders
- Leadership training experiences that are not required
- Reading and study
- Courses
- Groups for spiritual development
- Marriage and couples retreats
- Relationship seminars
- 12-step communities
- Personal trainers
- Spiritual directors
- Advanced degrees and education that is not required

When you see people who regularly submit themselves to these kinds of structure, not as an unusual occurrence, then you are looking at people whose orientation is toward growth. I know of one person who leads a consulting company that invests 10 percent of its gross revenues in R & D for the upper-level staff. They have it as a fund and spend it to bring in other experts in their industry, commission research, and for other things that are going to make them "more" than they are. As a result, their company has done some innovative things that have paid them back multifold for the investment.

So, take a look at your calendar and checkbook. Are you too tight with your time and money to grow? If you are, that is like a farmer who will not spend the money on seed or fertilizer. And, eventually, the field is going to be harvested out, and there is not going to be anything left to grow. The natural death is going to take over. But, if you are sowing to your growth through spending the necessary time and money to become more, then the future is going to pay you back for that aspect of your character.

It is the same thing that you see in businesses. The ones led by characters who will spend the money on R & D for both products and their people will explode in future years. They pass the competition who just continue to do business as usual. They have not only an eye for the future, but the character to go there before it comes to them. Their character *does not hold on, but is able to let go and spend for the future. Hoarders, and people who wish to always harvest and never relinquish some of the harvest for a future harvest, never grow.*

As Don Soderquist, former Vice Chairman and COO of Wal-Mart, reports in *The Wal-Mart Way*, "If an organization plans to promote people from within on a continuing basis, the associates need help in developing their God-given talent. In 1983, we launched the Walton Institute for the purpose of helping all levels of management in all divisions become better leaders. The purpose of the institute was not improving job skill but rather helping our people develop leadership and interpersonal skill" (*The Wal-Mart Way*, Soderquist, Thomas Nelson, 2005, pp. 68–69).

He then goes on to say that they regularly provided "schooling, mentoring by existing leaders (i.e., store managers, district managers, regional vice presidents, and so on), Dale Carnegie Training courses in the home office, evaluations focused on helping individuals grow, and a constant reminder and encouragement of the opportunities that existed at Wal-Mart" (p. 69). He also reports that they regularly passed out good books to thousands of their leaders and encouraged them to read, highlight, and review them.

## Submission to Someone Further Down the Road

Another aspect of growth characters is the ability to seek out and submit to "mentors," or people who are further down the road. They can take input, and modeling, and are not ashamed to ask for it. The ones who "know it all" or are somehow above asking or afraid to ask for help are the ones who hit the ceiling.

When you interview successful people, they will always be able to go back and see the major growth seasons of their lives being launched and guided by mentors. Some of these relationships were informal, and some more structured. But, virtually all people who leave good wakes have submitted themselves to the input of people "further down the road." And, the interesting thing is that they tend to do that for life, not just in the early years. They always value the experience of others and willingly take it in.

The relevant character aspects here have to do with the resistance to being known as one truly is. To be mentored means that we allow someone to look at all we are doing, our practices, our ignorance, our lack of ability, and to speak into that. That takes the ability to be vulnerable and open.

If someone has a lot of shame or narcissism (the wish to look ideal), then the mentoring turns into a time of hiding, or performing to look good. Arrogance or resistance to authority can do the

same. Being thin-skinned and unable to take feedback and direction can render a person "unmentorable." If we have the need to
look good, mentoring doesn't work because it requires our not
looking good, and coming clean with the need to grow. If we can't
do that, we are stuck where we are.

I remember one of the most important mentors I ever had, a su-
pervisor in my clinical training. He was brilliant and had vast clinical knowledge. I could learn more in an hour and a half with him
than I could from an entire semester with some other instructors. I
will always be grateful for what I learned, except there was a hitch
to it all.

He was sadistic. He took joy in revealing how stupid and igno-
rant graduate students and interns could be. He would relish getting to your weak areas, exposing them, and grinding it in. At times,
it was just horrible, and in supervision groups I remember feeling
awful for some people, as well as myself. But, *it was worth it.* The jew-
els of information and experience that he had to provide were
worth it all, but difficult to go through.

I remember heading for his office one day and a student coming
up to me and asking "How do you deal with that?" He had seen me
getting humiliated by this man more than once.

I said, "I just see it kind of like the price of something very valuable. What I learn from him is incredible, and what I pay for it is
the verbal abuse. So, before I walk in there, I just remind myself
that this is not the place to go looking for approval or kindness. I
am there to steal his knowledge and information, and if getting put
down is how I break into that safe, I will do it every time."

But I remember another student who said to me, "There is no
way I would be in his group. I refuse to subject myself to that. Who
needs it?" Made sense, and I usually think that it is good policy for
us to stay away from abusive people. But, what stood out to me was
that this guy was narcissistic and had to always be seen in a positive

light. So, he did not have the option or the choice of gaining good things from someone who was not going to coddle him and make him feel smart. *His need to feel good about himself overshadowed his drive to grow.* As a result, he just gravitated toward people who stroked him. I have followed his work for over twenty years and seen him gravitate from one thing to another that always had the same "feel good" and "seem smart and special" quality. He has never really gotten far with any of it, and none of it has developed into much. But, I am sure that he has felt comfortable along the way.

Growers will tell you that they have subjected themselves to tough coaches and mentors, endured the discomfort, and gained immensely through the process. They had to leave their need for comfort and happy talk at the door.

## Values the Present, Doesn't Want to Stay There

Characters who grow balance hunger and gratitude. They celebrate growth and victory. They know the meaning of the Jewish proverb "a desire accomplished is sweet to the soul." When they grow and accomplish something, it really matters to them. It is internalized as a good thing and becomes part of them, and they experience gratitude and appreciation for what has happened.

But, they don't sit there and rest on their laurels. Successful characters always have the drive to move on past the status quo. The others become "one-hit wonders."

The balance is important, as it gets to the dynamic of fulfillment. If people do not have the drive past the status quo, they do not create increase. But, if they cannot enjoy the present and what they have accomplished, they do not become sustainable. They burn out or become one-dimensional. On the one extreme is the lack of motivation, on the other extreme is the driven personality who will never get "there" because there is no "there" that is good enough to be of value.

The mature character loves today. She loves what today has accomplished. Her soul is satisfied when she looks at the result. She is grateful for the accomplishment, proud of it, and grateful to all of those who helped bring it about. She thanks them, rewards them, and celebrates with them. The process is as important as the goal. Then, tomorrow, she will strive for more.

## Subject Themselves to Their Inability

We talked earlier about not gambling, but taking risks that are natural extensions of growth. But just because something is a natural extension of growth does not mean that it is a slam dunk or someone just steps out and is able to do it. In fact, for growth to occur, by definition, the attempt has to be about something that you are not able to do. It has to be a "try."

People who grow jump in over their head. They try things that they cannot do, then stretch to become able to do what they are attempting. They take on challenges that ask them to become more than they have been or done before. Then the pressures of those demands call for them to become more in order to meet them. The bar is raised, and they have to jump higher. Here is the rule:

> You will not grow without attempting things
> you are unable to do.

To learn how to skydive, you have to jump out of the plane. To learn how to sell, you have to make some calls. To learn how to develop a better marriage, you have to try to do some things you have never done, such as open up, become vulnerable, or even confront.

We do not grow without some sort of necessary reach. That is why the ones who produce increase nearly always have clear goals and expectations that are written down. Then, they put themselves out there to reach them. Some of those are in areas where they are already capable, such as doing more of the same. But some of those are reaching at things never before attempted.

Going into new areas of endeavor, new markets, new positions, new responsibilities, new skills, are all aspects of growth. What is interesting about characters who grow in this way is their continual placement of themselves into the thin air of things never before attempted. They have the Indiana Jones experience that says, "I'm making this up as I go along."

When people get married for the first time, that reality bar is new, never before attempted. By definition, they don't know how to make it work. But, the having to make it work pushes them to grow and turn into the person who can make it work, if they put their arms around the challenge. If they don't, they don't make it. That is why a lot of marriages fail, *not because someone did not know how to make it work, but because they did not grow into the new challenge.*

No one is ready for parenting until she finds herself there and is *stretched into the person she has to become to meet that demand.* The being there turns people into that person, given the embracing of the challenge and the elements of growth that we have described. But, without taking the plunge, they wouldn't have grown into it. They might be able to teach it, but not to do it. So, the rule of growth that these characters perpetually practice is:

> They place themselves in situations that demand
> more of them than they are able to deliver.

A family-held oil company I know of had twenty-five years of successful operations by the founder, and slow, steady growth through the years, mainly achieved by maintaining business with growing companies. The founder made money mostly by growing with them, and increasing profits by improving processes. But, suddenly, at sixty, he died of a heart attack. His widow was only fifty and had never worked in the business. The accountants and management team told her that the wise move was to sell. She would be set for life and not have to deal with any hassles. But, that was not her.

Her life had been one of leaping into things that she had never done before and mastering them. She had been a national leader in philanthropic organizations and endeavors and had done a lot of work in the developing world. Her motto had almost been "If you already know how to do it, that's not what you should be doing." So, she decided to take over the reins of the company. She knew nothing about it, as her husband had always built a pretty tall wall around it and did not want her involved. He did not think she would "understand the business." But, she surprised everyone by achieving a lot of growth.

She did not "gamble," in the way we talked about above, in that she did not all of a sudden make a bunch of impulsive decisions. But she got engaged in the operations and learned the business by stepping into things she did not know how to do. It was overwhelmingly stretching, but she loved the ways it pushed her. Then, she started to break out of the shell, both of her husband's beliefs that she could not do it, as well as the shell of her previous experience.

The outcome was interesting. She found that she had a knack for it, and more than that, she loved the wheeling and dealing of it all. She expanded at a rate that the company had never done and led it to more growth than even her husband had, who was not as growth-oriented as she was. He was more defensive by nature and had always played conservative strategies that protected what he already had instead of looking for more.

## Rest

Another character aspect related to the ability to celebrate mentioned above is the ability to rest and recreate. In the same way that muscles require downtime to regenerate with stronger mass, so does the rest of our being. Your brain is designed to respond to the positive stress that growth demands place on it, and to benefit from those. But to have it overstimulated constantly does not allow it to do the replenishing that it needs.

The idea of a sabbatical has science behind it. In the same way, integrated people who have drive but are not "driven" are able to "Sabbath" and recreate. The idea of a Sabbath is a period of time (twenty-four hours weekly) where you are not producing anything. Rest means not producing. When something is not producing, it is regenerating. And while that is happening, good things are occurring that get it ready for the next production cycle. Fields need to lie fallow to restore fertility for future harvests.

To do this requires a character makeup that is capable of rest. Some people cannot be still and cannot rest. When they do, unresolved conflicts emerge; feelings of emptiness, fear, and other bothersome states bubble to the surface. To feel good about themselves or life, they have to be constantly producing. As a result, they are on perpetual output, and nothing is coming in or regenerating to make the future better. It will be linear and more of the same, until it begins to wind down and growth cannot occur.

## Helps Others Develop More

William Glasser, the psychiatrist who founded Reality Therapy, said that the best way to retain anything is to teach it. His research showed that the highest memory of material occurred when someone had to teach that material to others. Teaching and sharing is a growth experience.

What I find about those who grow in their own lives is that they are also always investing in the growth of others. They not only subject themselves to mentors and people further down the road than they are, but they are also the ones further down the road for someone else. They give away what they possess and invest in others becoming more.

I have a partner who was part of the management group that bought Coldwell Banker Residential. At the time he first went there, it was owned by Sears and was losing a lot of money. His task was to turn it around. One of the first things that he surmised was that it needed to grow its people and its leaders. That is where he put his focus, even more than on the "nuts and bolts of the business." It began to turn around. Then, Sears decided to get rid of it, and so confident that he could grow it, he and four managers partnered and bought it with outside investment and debt totaling $150 million. Being oriented toward growth himself, one of his primary focuses continued to be to grow the leaders. They invested in helping others develop. They had established Coldwell Banker University for leadership training, seeing the development of their people as the best thing that they could do to grow the company.

Now here is the magic. One year later, they paid the $100 million back that they had borrowed and, three years later, sold the company for $650 million. It was a great turnaround story, but one in large part fueled by the investment in the growth and development of their people. Where did this come from? From a business-strategy book?

It came from the *character* of the principals. The one who drove it was just executing the pattern that he has always executed as part of his makeup. Beginning as a mentor of youth in high school and college, he continued to see helping others develop as just another part of being alive. Along the way, it turned into hundreds of millions in profit, but that was not the reason it was there. It was there as an aspect of his character.

Now, ten years later, you can find him doing the same thing. He gathers young businesspeople under his wing who he thinks are doing interesting and helpful things that have social value and mentors them in how to do whatever they are doing better. His two guiding questions are always "Why are you doing what you are doing?" and "How can you do it better?" Growth is motivated by the right "whys" and by growing into someone who can do that better. But, for him, business strategy was not what led him into growth. Growth led his business strategy. It was an expression of character. He must build into other people growing as well as himself. It is just a part of who he is.

## Integration Reveals Itself

Our view of character has been based on the importance of integration at the macro level. The big picture is where all the aspects of character are whole and come together to make for a person who is "all together." But in the micro level of this aspect, integration is a telltale sign of character as well. The person who is doing it well is growing not in just one area of life, but all of them. That is the way that you know it is character and not compensation.

Some people just focus on their career, for example, and create lopsided growth. While they grow that aspect of who they are, the rest of their lives lags behind. The fruit shows the neglect of an integrated focus of growth. They advance in their profession and lose a marriage. They win accolades, but because of spiritual emptiness end up wondering, "What was it all for?" They become technically savvy, and relationally inept.

When growth is like that, it is often compensatory in that people rely on a strength to become all of life. In that way, they are asking that aspect of themselves to do things that it cannot do. Your work cannot fulfill all of your needs as a person. Nor can your relationships. But, often when people have character conflicts in one of those areas, they will ask the other area to become their whole life and thus compensate for what they can't do well. That is imbalance, and it always leaves its own wake.

The integrated character feels the same hunger and awareness of the drive in all areas, the relational, spiritual, intellectual, and other aspects. In that, they create balance, and growth in one area fuels growth in another. Lopsided growth is a symptom of some aspect of disintegration in the person.

So, putting it all together means that for growth to happen, people are fully alive, hungry for more, and not afraid to go out and seek it. In the seeking, in all areas, they become more than they were yesterday and pass that on.

VII

# CHARACTER DIMENSION SIX

## Oriented Toward Transcendence

# 12

## when you're small, you're bigger

there is an old story about a navy warship that was heading through the fog one night when a distant, faint light appeared directly in their heading. As they continued, it got brighter, and the captain walked to the helm to assess the situation. About that time, a voice came over the radio and said, "Attention. Calling the vessel traveling eighteen knots on a 220 heading, adjust your course thirty degrees, immediately."

The captain got on the radio and responded, "This is the vessel on the 220 heading. You adjust your course thirty degrees."

"Negative, Captain. You adjust," came the reply.

"I am an admiral in the United States navy," said the commander. "Who am I speaking to?"

"I am an ensign in the U.S. Coast Guard."

"Then, I suggest you adjust your course."

"No, sir. I suggest that you adjust yours."

"We are a U.S. navy warship," said the admiral. "You adjust."

"We are a lighthouse," said the ensign.

Some things are just bigger than we are. But that doesn't mean that we always *know* that they are. We can think that we are the bigger ship, and that whatever is in the way of what we want should get out of the way and adjust. Many times, that is true, and that kind of perseverance can be at the heart of much performance. We have pointed out, for example, that integrated character pushes against obstacles and finds a way to overcome them in order to achieve.

But, some things are not going to move, and we are the smaller ship that must adjust our course and steer in a different direction if we are going to make it. If we do, we find a heading that works, and we make it to our destination. But, if we can't see that reality, we break ourselves against it. We hit the wall, and it breaks us.

Whether or not we believe in gravity, for example, it exists. It is bigger than we are. It transcends us. And, like the lighthouse, it invites us to adjust our course to its reality. If we do, we fit into its reality and do well. We can even use it to our advantage. Engineers study it and find ways to go with it, designing planes that work within it and the other laws of physics, and we benefit. But, if they ignore those transcendent laws, the planes go down. We can push the limits all we want, thinking they will move, but ultimately we will bow to them.

> To live and flourish, we must bow
> to the things larger than us.

Seems like common sense, right? And that is where character enters the scene and will determine everything about a person's wake.

## The Big Question

As a psychologist, I would have to say that one question hovers above all others in importance for a person's functioning in life. It is the question "Are you God, or not?" The way that a person answers that one determines everything else that we have been talking about in character and functioning.

On the surface, it seems to be a little bit silly, in that most people, especially leaders, can check the right box when that question comes up on a test. If they don't, we have medication, straitjackets, and locked hospital units to help them deal with the reality they are going to encounter if they believe they are in charge of the universe. We call it psychosis.

So, most people will answer the question correctly. "Of course I am not God," they say. But, if you follow them around, they spend the rest of the time *acting as if they are.* They live as if they are the center of the universe and that everything and everyone exist to serve them and their purposes. They put all of their efforts into building their own little kingdom, whether that is their household, a company, their relationships, or their interests. They feel as if it all revolves around them, and that the lighthouse should move. They experience themselves as the center of their universe.

In its worst forms, this is the ultimate sickness, akin to what psychologists refer to as narcissism. It is marked by such traits as grandiosity, omnipotence, extreme selfishness, exploitiveness, an overestimation of one's talents or importance, feelings of entitlement, and egocentricity. People feel they are "special." You know the traits and have seen them. Descriptions of them make it into the vernacular of our culture, such as T-shirts that say, "It's all about me."

But, aside from such jokes that more normal people make about themselves when they see themselves as a little self-centered, most of the time we do not like the trait at all and do not want to be identified with it in any manner. We see it as immature at best, and arrogant, selfish, or prideful at worst. Self-centeredness is not admirable, paradoxically, as the ones who possess it often crave the very admiration that their character does not earn.

The opposite of this kind of self-centeredness can be described in a lot of different ways. I like to think of it as the quality of "transcendence." It is the person who has gotten beyond, above, or transcended ordinary human selfishness and self-centeredness and lives in a very different reality from thinking life revolves around him or her. She realizes that there are things much bigger than her, and that her existence is really not just about her and her interests, but ultimately about the things larger than she is. Her life is about fitting into those things, joining them, serving them, obeying them, and finding her role in the big picture. Then, as a result, she ultimately becomes a part of them and finds meaning much larger than a life that is just about her. Life is about things that transcend her.

## Bigger Than Me

It is not only the megalomaniacs and those with Napoléon complexes who think it is all exists for them. There are milder versions as well, and those are the ones that we usually battle within ourselves, and in people whom we associate with. Often this trait is just annoying, but if someone has a lot of responsibility, or if we are connected to him in a significant way, the results can be devastating.

Instead, we long to be around the ones who throw themselves into the task and the mission of the greater good. They see the bigger picture and become part of a team. You can see it in their reactions to things, as they do not view the situation as being all about them, or existing only to serve them and their needs. How about this example: The leader brings everyone in and tells them that there is a great opportunity for the company and for everyone who belongs to it. A new market has opened up, and to develop the capacity to conquer it, they are going to have to move to a new facility. "We have to get lean and mean," she says. "But it is going to be so great. We are going to blow our previous goals through the ceiling and accomplish our mission in such a bigger way. Our dreams are going to multiply. It is more than we could have imagined."

You can feel the excitement in the room, as the team comes together more than ever around this bigger purpose and goal. Spirits, visions, and expectations are lifted. Then, right in the middle of the enthusiasm, someone raises his hand and says, "But, does this mean I am going to lose my window office? I was told I would have a window. If we move, I don't want to lose it."

The air goes out of the room. You want to scream, "It's not about you, or your stupid window! It is about things bigger than you. Get over it."

The big things, not ourselves, are the things that make us big. As we join them, we become larger. The paradox is that to join things bigger than us, we have to humble ourselves and become "smaller," in a sense. When we realize that we are smaller than the transcendent things, and we exist for *them* and not them for *us,* we grow into greatness. The greatest people are the ones who have not sought greatness, but served greatly the causes, values, and missions that were much bigger than them. And by joining and serving those, we see greatness emerge.

But, if we think we are "bigger," and that everything is about us, then we are reduced to a little world of our own making. And we see everything only in terms of what it means for us. The results are always either shallow, smaller, or even toxic, destructive, and poisonous. As Thomas Merton said, "To consider persons and events and situations only in the light of their effect upon myself is to live on the doorstep of hell."

## Things That Are Bigger

So what are the "bigger things"? What are the lighthouses? There are many, some of which are universally accepted, and some we choose to value. My purpose here is not to choose for you what the bigger things worth "bowing" to are for you. My purpose here is for us to look at the character trait of being *able* to bow to them, and being *willing* to bow to them, more than defining what those things are. The things that one of us holds transcendent may not be as big for someone else, and vice versa. But, at the same time, most of the civilized world agrees on some universals and absolutes that we should bow to, and we can learn from them.

One category of things that transcend us are values. Values form a lot of the architecture of a person's character, his shape and personhood. They do the same thing for an organization, or a relationship. What we value is what we esteem or put above all else, including our self-interests, and then guide our behavior from that heading. If a boss or a company values employees and people as well as profits, then he or it will bow to the demands of that value, even at the expense of his own self-interest. If a company values the environment, it will behave in ways that are at the expense of just gaining "more profit." It won't cut corners. If a person values his or her family, then he or she makes choices that "cost" his or her self-interests, or career interests, in order to serve the greater good that is valued.

But, if he or she values him- or herself above all else, then when there is a conflict, the self always wins. If a company values its own interests above all else, then the other things take a backseat. The problem is that when we are dealing with these timeless, universal values, they are like lighthouses. They do not get out of the way, and the person or the company ultimately crashes upon their reality. Universal values such as love, compassion, justice, freedom, honesty, faithfulness, responsibility, and the like are not really "optional" any more than gravity. We can choose to ignore them and not bow to them, but if we do, there are inevitably consequences.

This is what happened in the huge corporate meltdowns in recent years. When a few people valued themselves and their own interests as the *ultimate* interest, the ultimate reality, then everything was there to serve them. This is the egocentric behavior that says "I am God" and "It all exists to serve me" or "I am the center and it revolves around and adapts to what I want," as opposed to "I exist to serve the things that are bigger than me." In the end, they found that there are things bigger than their own interests, and that by getting it wrong, they wreaked huge damage. Their wake was enormous. They left serious damage behind not only for themselves, but for the very things larger than them as well. And, they lost their own interests as well. The paradox always holds true. Give up things for yourself, and you get more. Seek only yourself, and you will lose even what you have.

In their egocentricity, just thinking about themselves, these people forgot some big things that transcended them and their interests. They did not think about how what they were doing would affect the stockholders, the employees, the investors and the markets, the business partners, values and accepted ethics, long-standing accounting principles, governments, people's retirements, the trust of the nation, and the economy itself. These are the bigger things, the bigger realities. They did not bow to those reality de-

mands, but instead did "off-balance-sheet deals," funny accounting, and lots of other irregularities. They ignored ethics and values.
As a result, they brought down many of the things that were larger
than them, and everyone suffered as they learned why those transcendent realities are in fact reality. You cannot ignore the transcendent things and expect all to come out well. Gravity and
lighthouses have the last say.

By looking out for only themselves, they dealt a devastating
blow on the ability of the entire markets to function. They destroyed trust. No investors, private or institutional, wanted to put
money in anything because they could no longer trust the numbers.
The integrity of long-respected companies was undermined by this
lack of transcendence, as well as the integrity of the markets themselves. Legislation had to be passed to make executives more accountable for the wake that their lack of transcendence created.
The interesting result is that remedies, such as the Sarbanes-Oxley
reform, end up being debated by business leaders, who say that it
will take up a lot of time and resources that are needed for other
things and not solve the problem of corporate shenanigans.

*That is the point.* Laws exist to fill in the gap and police the failure
of character. They really are a "backup" system. But laws can never
do what the integrity of values can do. If someone is honest, and the
numbers are trustworthy, then extra effort to make sure those are
accurate is not needed. Character is on the watch. But, if character
is not there, then laws are all we have to throw at the problem.
Government regulation basically comes from the lack of self-
regulation. You put kids in time-out only because they misbehave.
It is a sad thing to think of all of the great industries that have been
marginalized by abuses of individuals in the system. Henry Silver-
man was the CEO of Cendant during the rocky times of corporate
shakeups a few years ago. After Cendant paid billions to settle lawsuits, he said:

> "[*The new regulations*] *are kind of like chicken soup. They can't cure you—but can't hurt you either. There will always be fraud in the world. I don't know how you regulate human behavior, which is what these rules are trying to do.*"
>
> *When asked what would prevent bad behavior, he responded:*
>
> "*Individual mores and ethics of the leaders at companies, and their ability to instill what's right and what's wrong. We had a biannual meeting where all of the senior managers came to the New York office. I made a point to talk about integrity. I said: 'If there's something you'd prefer not to read about on the front page of the* Wall Street Journal, *then just don't do it.' Most companies, I'm afraid, haven't instilled that culture in their troops.*"
>
> (BusinessWeek *Online, July 31, 2002*)

There is only one true "regulator," and that is a person's character integrity when it is oriented towards transcendence.

When I was in the psychiatric-hospital industry, we used to actually have the opportunity to put someone in the hospital and give him or her the treatment that was needed. Imagine that. When I first started, our average length of stay, for example, was about thirty days. In thirty days, you can do a lot to get to the root of someone's addiction or depression or family issues. You can diagnose and treat the underlying medical and biological issues as well. You can make significant directional changes in the entire path of people's lives. Massive amounts of research showed the cost benefits of treatment to companies, individuals, and anyone who had an economic interest in their well-being. Now, twenty years later, I still get letters and run into former patients who say, "That month changed my life. Everything is on a totally different path now. It was the most significant thing that ever happened to me."

But, over time, things changed. There were so many abuses in that industry that the money to pay for that kind of treatment went away, and the trust in the system eroded as well. Insurance companies could not trust some doctors or hospitals. I remember seeing the abuses by some hospitals and doctors, keeping patients for months when they did not need it or it was even contraindicated. But, as long as they could bill the insurance company and get paid, they kept them. Over time, the system broke down, and insurance companies reacted. I remember when it started to happen and I would try to hospitalize someone who really needed it. "We will give you three days," the insurer would say, "and then we want her out."

"What? Are you joking?" we would retort. "We will barely have stabilized her in three days. She needs a lot more than that, even to get the meds right."

"Sorry, that's all you're getting," would be the comeback. "That should be plenty."

I would have to inform the patient that even if we were willing to drastically discount our fees, the hospital could not keep her, and we were not going to be able to do more than just get her stable and then she had to go somewhere else. It would be heartbreaking, as it still is today. At first glance, it would be easy to hate the insurance company, blaming their greed. But it was more than greed on their parts. It was also the problem of their not being able to trust the system. There were breakdowns on both sides, and in the end everyone lost. Throw the greedy malpractice attorneys into the mix (not the good ones), and the risk ratio gets even worse. And the "bigger things," such as having good treatment that makes individuals, families, and even their jobs survive, are lost. *In part, because people milked the system for what they could get out of it, without thinking of the bigger picture.* They did not bow to the things that transcended them, so they lost everything.

Anything of value can be brought down by enough individuals

who do not bow to the larger things. A family can be brought down by a spouse who does not bow to the bigger issue of faithfulness, rather than his own immediate gratification in an affair. A business can be brought down by not bowing down to the bigger picture of the customers' needs or the employees', or their values. As Jim Collins made clear in *Built to Last,* it is the companies that live out their values who win in the long run. That is true about individuals as well. Character always wins.

## Awareness

The first aspect of character that affects transcendence is awareness. The ones who live for the bigger things know that bigger exists. They are aware. The ones who don't are just on autopilot, mainly driven by their hungers, passions, and desires for gratification. In Freudian terms, they are guided by their instinctual impulses, looking for a socially acceptable way to feed themselves. But, fortunately, as we all know, a lot of people have transcended that animal-like state. They have become "aware" or enlightened that there are bigger things than themselves and their appetites.

They have what psychologists refer to as an ego ideal that they pursue, which is in part constructed with aspects of conscience and consciousness that guide them to higher levels of living, behavior, and achievement past "feeling good." Love, service, justice, and their guiding principles live there, as well as a motivation to achieve them and a sense of fulfillment when they do. Their awareness leads to real action, but the awareness comes first.

What I see about characters who have this kind of ideal is that they have gone through some sort of process to get there and mold those ideals. Some of it is their parenting, but not all of it. Some of it is having gone through the hard knocks, or "hit bottom," where the importance of these things was learned. Alcoholics, for example, often go through an enlightenment when they lose a relationship(s) or career or something else important as a result of their addiction. They see that just feeding themselves can destroy everything important to them. So, they get it, after they hit a lighthouse.

Others "catch" awareness from being around leaders and other people who have been enlightened themselves. They are inspired. The contrast between themselves and these inspirational models wakes them out of their slumber. They can no longer face themselves with their shallow existence as deep calls to deep.

Still others are forced to look past themselves not from hitting bottom, but from reaching "the end of themselves." There is an emptiness, a lack of meaning, or just a goal that cannot be reached. Their path does not get them to a place that is fulfilling or is working. They realize that "there must be more" to get them to some perceived goal or state, or to life itself. As a result, they seek transcendence. It is still a choice to grow, as we saw in the last section, but the choice is propelled by a need for something more.

Then there is the dissatisfaction of the people who love them that sometimes propels them to look past themselves. They might not yet have lost the relationship, but someone in their life is pushing for more from them than the self-centered existence that they are living. The stance that it is "all about me" is leaving out the "we" that includes the other, whether the "other" is the spouse, kids, or other significant people. Those people press the person to wake up and get it.

However someone gets past his own self-centered existence, becoming aware that there is more, or a greater good, is the first step. The next step is to try to find out what that "more" is about. Sometimes this propels people into some sort of metaphysical search that is really not transcendent at all, in that it is still about themselves. It seems to be transcendent in that it is about more than their day-to-day physical and material needs, but upon close inspection it is still about being caught up in themselves. Some forms of meditation, for example, do not propel people into greater involvement and service of things bigger than themselves, but are just an attempt to be "bigger than themselves," as they seek to lose themselves in some impersonal force or deity and become one with it. It is still primitive narcissism in that it really does not involve an "other" that results in a meaningful investment of the self in someone or something "else," which is the only way to grow. Instead, these attempts at transcendence are just one more kind of gratification of the self and do not propel people forward.

But the people who truly emerge from themselves do that by getting out of themselves and investing themselves in things larger. For some that is a faith, for others a cause or service, a mission, or just values that cause them to pour themselves out to others in greater and more diverse ways. As they do, they are enlarged. Look around your office and see the ones who give time and effort to a cause, versus the ones who can only look at their portfolio numbers over and over. Whom do you want to be?

## Self-Denial, Self-Correction, and the Ability to Adjust

The real indicator of this kind of character is whether it shows up in behavior. It is one thing to hold to values or principles of great significance, but it is a totally different matter to have those appear on the easel of life. Just as "faith without works is dead," values without visible expression of those in time and space are not worth much more than an intellectual exercise and do little to affect the wake of someone's life. If we want to know what we value, then we have to look at how we spend our time, money, energy, etc. In other words, where our treasure is, there our heart is also.

So, it begins with investment. It doesn't begin with just saying we care about something. It has to be exercised, and internalized. But like all internalizations or growth, the structure of the patterns have to be exercised first, both to wean oneself from the pull of the shallow existence that is comfortable, as well as find the realization of the fulfillment of the deeper life. If you never stop eating potato chips to try a steady diet of healthy food, you will never realize the true change of taste that happens when you eat what your body was designed to eat. But after you do, and sustain it, you can never go back, other than for an occasional holiday binge that ultimately your system rejects and you find yourself longing to be back on the wagon.

People who develop this kind of transformation and sustain it do it with a structured approach, at least in the beginning. They take a class, get a spiritual director or mentor, volunteer in an organization, join a growth group, or find some other path that has a structure to it. When they do that, and it includes the elements of awareness, a template, stretching experiences, practice, correction, feedback, and the other elements of growth we talked about, in the last section, it slowly becomes their own. Then they might morph the structures to fit their own style or needs or even launch out into something new. But, first, they submit to some structured growth path to stretch themselves and mold this aspect of their being.

The more that they adapt and submit themselves to that structure, the more that they see aspects of themselves that are not as transcendent as they once thought. They are humbled and see the need to grow even more. The task that they are about gets them in touch with both the enormity of the need that they have given themselves to, as well as their own inadequacies to meet that need or to measure up to the path of the ones who have gone before them.

When they give to the poor, if they are really developing transcendent character, they move past the ones who only have a feeling of "Gee, I did a good thing. That feels really good. I am a good person," which the occasional givers have. They move on to a deeper internalization of serving the "bigger things." It is not about "being good," another self-motivated way of thinking. It becomes more and more a way of being that is not about the self at all. The person is fulfilled in the meaning that is derived in doing good past its making him a "good person." It is intrinsic. In a way, there is more and more "ego death," as the masters have referred to it, and more connection to the higher transcendent values. Mother Teresa was fulfilled in helping the bigger cause, not looking in the mirror and thinking what a good person she was.

At this point, there is a new "addictive cycle," not to seeking more and more for oneself and never being satisfied, but to giving more and more of oneself and becoming more satisfied than one thought possible. It is the difference in the amount of "happiness" that a child experiences on Christmas morning, or by going to Disneyland, having all of those gifts or experiences for him- or herself, versus the incredible joy that his or her parent feels in getting to give that experience to the child. It truly is more blessed to give than to receive. The ones who give of themselves know this and love the experience. But, all of this begins with an investment, and usually one that involves submitting to a structured path.

I have a friend who is like this, and he structures it for his company as well, to introduce people to the process. They have periodic "give back" days to the community where the employees select a charity, and the entire company volunteers to descend on that charity with all of its resources and do whatever they can. It may be a re-

vamp of the IT department, or a remodel. With several hundred
employees, you can do a lot. What he says happens is that people
who have never thought of things bigger than themselves "get the
bug" from submitting to that structure and go from there to developing a more values-centered life.


## Tylenol and Other Lessons

What does transcendent character look like when the rubber meets
the road? Take the transcendent leadership shown in the Tylenol
crisis of 1982. Johnson & Johnson learned that people had died
after taking Tylenol and, as the investigation unfolded, further discovered that some of its bottles had been removed from the shelves,
laced with cyanide, and put back. At the time, Tylenol accounted
for a huge percentage of Johnson & Johnson's profits and was the
leader in painkillers. It outsold many of its competitors combined.
So, this crisis was a huge blow to Johnson & Johnson. What were
they to do?

It was only a few bottles, some could have reasoned, limited to
the area of Chicago. What were the real risks of widespread danger?
This was probably one deranged person who had limited ability to
inflict more harm past what he or she had already done. In some
companies, you could have found the numbers guys adding up the
liability of a few bad outcomes, and concluding that the profits
would still be strong even if they had to pay out some liabilities.
Keep it on the shelves, and if something bad happens, that is what
insurance is for. There have been many instances of that kind of
reasoning, where a company puts its self-interests above everything
else.

But, not here. The company put a strategy together that put itself and the product down the list of priorities past the "bigger
thing": "How can we protect the people?" Regardless of the costs,

they figured that one death was too many to risk. They immediately pulled Tylenol off the shelves in Chicago and, soon thereafter, pulled it totally off the market. *They removed it from every shelf in the United States.*

That is transcendent action. It is one thing to say that one of your values is people, or customer safety. It is another to take the strongest product of your company and stop selling it to save one person. That is the right thing to do. This is different from any "cost-benefit" analysis of things which are good. Car accidents kill people, as do some maloccurances of medications. But cars and those meds are good things which have some bad side effects. The value is to help. Here, cyanide poisoning was preventable, and not part of any good thing. There were other pain meds available, so the higher value said "pull it."

Following Hurricane Katrina, it was encouraging and lifting to the spirit to see businesses connect to the transcendent value of helping others in a time of need. The Louisiana Department of Health and Hospitals reported the following on their Web site:

"The Louisiana Board of Pharmacy has received confirmation that emergency prescription needs will be taken care of for Hurricane Katrina evacuees without means to pay for their medications. Evacuees can go to any Wal-Mart, CVS, Rite Aid, Walgreen's or Kroger's pharmacy in Louisiana or around the country to have their emergency prescriptions filled at no cost *depending upon patient need.* Nurses and doctors who have authority to write prescriptions and are treating patients in special needs shelters as part of the recovery effort can send their patients' prescriptions to these pharmacies to be filled."

That is transcendent action again, doing things that cost these companies, but for the greater good. The bigger values dictated their behavior.

That is the next issue after being aware of transcendent realities

and internalizing them into one's character in some structured setting. It is the bending of the knee, the bowing to those bigger
things, *when no one is making you or no one is watching* that means they are
real. Tylenol makers could have gathered in a boardroom and as-
sessed the risk with the guiding principle of saving themselves and
doing damage control. While they certainly had to worry about
how to save the product and the company, that was not their first
concern. When no one was yet making them, they did the right
thing. And in the end, they won big-time. The public trusted them
and remained loyal. And the business world applauded them as a
model of trustworthiness and leadership.

So the question is what makes this kind of character able to do
that? Several things, but the first is really about the heart, and what
really matters to someone. When you do the right thing, it is usually
going to cost you and you are going to lose something. And it is difficult to sustain loss for something you don't really care about. Ultimately it is what someone really cares about that she or he is willing
to lose something for.

If Johnson & Johnson had not really cared about people, they
would not have been willing to go through the losses. It had to be in
the true fabric of the leadership. If leaders do not care about the
employees, then they will not institute policies that help them if
there is a cost. But if they do, they will be willing to lose some things
for that value. If a parent loves a child, he or she gives up things and
loses them for the development of the child.

So, love powers these values, but love is not enough. Ask any
couple who has hit a rough spot and one of them bailed and did not
make the hard choices to work it through. Past love, it takes the
willingness to exercise probably the greatest thing that integrated
character does: *self-denial*. You can love someone or a value or a mission or a purpose, but until you have denied yourself something
that you value for the sake of the other, then love is not enough.

Self-denial is always about loss. It is the willingness to lose something that truly matters to us for the service of something bigger.

This aspect of character is the basis of all that makes the world
go round, and when it breaks down, so goes the world. A mother
gives up comfort and energy that she does not have to get up one
more time for an infant. An adult gives up time, money, leisure, or
energy to take in or take care of an aging parent. A soldier or police
officer risks her life for her country or neighbor. In all of these acts,
there is loss, all the way to the loss of life.

So, to value the right things is a beginning. To make choices that
cost us to serve them is the end. But, as Tylenol's makers found out,
the end of oneself, the end of self-interest, is the beginning of an
even greater self. You win in the end by losing in the beginning, if
you lose to the more important things.

## Making the Shifts

I know a man who runs the western United States for one of the big
telecommunications companies. He is a transcendent character,
and a transcendent leader. To him, life, leadership, and business are
all about the "bigger things." One day, I asked him how he practices
his values in his company.

"Well," he said, "I just believe that businesses succeed when the
people are becoming the best that they can be and learn how to
come together to be the best that they can be together. So, at the beginning of the year, I always take my team of direct reports on a retreat and we begin with a few questions. The first is 'What would we
like to see happen in the next year?' That gets us to our vision, and
the goals. And we came up with a major one. We said we wanted to
do so well that the whole company would stop and want to know
how we did it. Pretty audacious, to say the least, that kind of goal.

"But, everyone has goals. It is the next steps that count. We then ask ourselves these questions: 'For those things to happen, what kind of team do we have to become? And how do each of us need to change to make that happen?'

"What happens at that point is it always *forces us to what our values are going to be and how we are going to live those out* in our relationships. For example, we realize that to reach those kinds of goals, we have to value teamwork and get rid of territorial pettiness. That means that we are going to have to trust each other and communicate. It means that sometimes we are going to have to drop what we are doing and go help the other ones fix something. It means that we are going to have to listen and care about each other and support one another."

"That's awesome," I said. "How has it gone?"

"So unbelievable. Last year, we painted quite a vision and then went to work on making the shifts in ourselves to living out those values. And we blew the doors off of all records in all the categories and led the country by far. We did so well that the CEO called to say they wanted to fly out and find out what we do that is different than everyone else, and how everyone else could learn it. *Exactly what our vision was!"* This leader was beaming, but you could tell it was a beam about how proud he was for the transcendence of it all, for their growth, and not just the numbers. He loved that the team got to the bigger issues and made the shifts that they needed to make to get there."

It is this "making the shifts" that counts. I think of it this way, as we have looked at earlier, but is illustrated by this team:

> The immature character asks life to meet
> his demands. But the mature character
> meets the demands of life.

The vision demanded that these individuals make shifts in their practices to meet the demands of the values. They did not ask the values to shift, but they did the shifting. When push came to shove, they gave up pettiness and competitiveness for helping each other, sharing information, and trust. They gave in to the demand of the value.

This is the mark of character that truly meets the demands of reality. When reality calls, they change whatever it takes to meet that demand. If what they are thinking of doing is not good for the bigger value, or the greater good, they make the shift and join the bigger, transcendent reality. They make the shift that they need to make.

As we said earlier, what those values are for any given person is a personal choice that only he or she can make. We all ultimately pick what we are going to value and serve. I do believe that there are some universal absolutes that are akin to gravity, and if we ignore those, we will crash, as mentioned above. The more we adjust to them, the better. Other values are more individual, to a person or to an organization. But, what is true about both the universal and the personal is that no matter what those values are, the character must be able and willing to bend in deference to them. For our purposes here, that is the issue.

A person with integrated character is a person who possesses the awareness that it is not all about him or her, and the ability and willingness to make the necessary adjustments to the things that transcend him or her at any given juncture. If people do that, then their wake in both their tasks and relationships is going to be bigger and better for everyone concerned. When the crucibles of testing come, in their work life, their marriage, their personal lives, or for the organization they lead, they will be able to meet the demands of reality because they are in touch with reality. It is not just about them.

# CONCLUSION

# where did it go?

"So what do you do?" I asked the guy assigned to my foursome in the charity golf tournament.

"I am a HR consultant," he said, "and I work with people in leadership and who run large companies. What about you?"

"I do some of that too, but a little bit more from the personal side than the usual leadership content. I am a psychologist, so I work with a lot of leaders in their individual development, you know, the issues-that-get-in-the-way kind of thing."

"Oh, gosh," he said. "It amazes me sometimes how really talented people in leadership are not very well prepared on the personal side. It is incredible. I just had a situation where a CEO had to fire someone who headed up an entire continent for a multinational electronics corporation, so he asked me to coach him in how to do it well. He thought it was going to be a difficult situation and wanted some help. So I flew out to meet with him and we went over all the issues, told him what to say, and the whole bit. I really prepared him well."

"So, what happened?" I asked.

"Well, I am about to leave, and he asks me if I will drive with him on his trip to meet the guy so, before he talks to him, we can have some more time to go over it. I thought it was a little overkill, but, hey, I was there to help, so I said OK.

"So, we drive there, about two hours, and all along the way he is asking me how to say this or that, what to do if the other guy says this or that or gets upset or whatever. I was beginning to see that in some way these questions were really not that difficult or technical . . . he could have figured out what to say, I think. I began to get the picture that he was just nervous about the confrontation, kind of going over the same ground over and over again. It just didn't make sense. He was a powerful guy, in terms of business and accomplishment. But he seemed kind of scared about this one."

"So, what happened then?" I asked. "Did he do it well?"

"That's where it gets really amazing. I drive there with him, talk it through, and then we get to the company. He asks me to come up to the suite with him, I am figuring just for moral support out in the waiting room, right? But that's not what happened."

"What did he do?" At this point I could almost feel the drama.

"We get to the door of the conference room where the guy is going to meet him, and I am about to wish him well and go sit somewhere, when he says, 'You do it.' He wanted me to go in and fire the guy."

"You are kidding me! And this guy is the CEO?"

"Yep. And a seemingly strong one, or at least I thought."

"So you know what I mean when I say that their 'issues' can get in the way," I said.

"More than most people. It is just incredible how truly com-

petent people can have such chinks in the armor. But, hey, it is
true."

As we have seen throughout this book, accomplished, experienced,
and admired high achievers can also have what this consultant
called the "chinks in the armor." But if we do not work closely with
them, we only see the good stuff. The degrees, the position, the assumed success, are what is easily visible. The other things don't
show up unless you are truly in the "wake." But, as we all know and
have experienced, the chinks are there, even in good, high achievers. The question is why? How does this happen? How can someone be so accomplished and yet have such significant personal
issues that sometimes really get in the way? Where do they come
from?

Having now seen what character is, and what its absence looks
like, let's take a look at why we have those character "chinks" so that
moving forward, you can do a few very powerful things:

1. Understand why you might have some "gaps" to work on
2. Accept yourself and realize that there is nothing "wrong"
   with having gaps
3. Know what to do next to resolve them

## Being Human, Superhuman, and Dysfunctional All at Once

It is something we all do. Whether you call it idealization, splitting,
naïveté, or the old "putting someone up on a pedestal," it is the tendency to see people as if they are only their strengths. This man was
the CEO of a multinational company. That is a lot of talent and accomplishment in a person. So we assume that he is just all that. We
hardly ever immediately think that someone with those kinds of

credentials is a human with weaknesses just like everyone else. So, we get caught off guard.

Worse than that, however, is that since we have a tendency to see others in that way, without weaknesses, fears, and insecurities, we secretly feel worse about our own. When we encounter some aspect of our own imperfections, we assume that no one who is accomplished could have *that* issue. "I must be a real loser or something" is the natural thinking that you have when you idealize others. And that kind of thinking makes it worse, because then you tend to *hide the areas where you have the greatest opportunity for growth.* As a result, you try to operate only using your strengths and thereby compensate for those weak areas in some way. Also, this "faking it" cycle gets worse as time goes on as the demands increase. Now you have a greater position and more people looking at you, so there is more pressure to look as if you have it all together. As a result, two things happen.

You are hiding more and therefore not working on the areas that need growth, and you are also getting further indoctrinated in the view of the world that people who are achievers don't have big holes inside them. "They don't lack things in their character. They really are as strong as they look," you think. And so the world turns, with more and more issues of really talented people going unaddressed and underdeveloped. And those unresolved issues are the ones that end up preventing you from getting where you want to go.

Even worse, sometimes people think that it is the lack of development that got someone to the place where he is. I hear this all the time when people talk about leadership character. They say, "Well, it is his drivenness and dictator personality that made him so successful. It is a problem in that it makes him difficult to work with, but without it he would not be where he is." *Wrong!* What they are calling "drivenness" means an unbalanced achiever who is aggressive about getting the goals accomplished, but absolutely immature or terrible in working with people, or so narcissistic that he is un-confrontable and has a "God complex."

That is *not* what made him successful. It is what created the collateral damage along his path toward success. His initiative, assertiveness, good use of being aggressive, brains, charm, strategic thinking, and other things made him successful, *in spite of the imbalance and narcissism, not because of it.* If he integrated those aspects of his character as well, the good ones that made him successful *would not disappear!* They would be augmented by other skills and make him even more powerful, not less. There often seems to be a fear against becoming a balanced person, *as if accomplishment only belongs to the truly dysfunctional.*

But the truth is, and this is really good news, that *every human being is to some degree unintegrated.* We all lack integrity in the ways that we are talking about in this book. We all can grow. But to do that we have to understand that the idealization of accomplished people, whereby we think they don't have struggles and weaknesses as we do, is a fantasy. You have to get over the fantasy that there are perfectly "together" people and join the community of growers, whereby we all realize that we are humans who all have a "next step" to take in our growth. We all have talents, even superhuman ones at times, and weaknesses and dysfunctions. The trick is to embrace those and become people and organizations that have a mentality of "imperfect stars who are getting better." The more that stance can become your personal and organizational culture, the more everyone is going to achieve.

## Where It Comes From

Where do these areas of incompleteness come from? Why can't you just get your MBA and assume that you are a grown-up ready to take on the world?

This book does not attempt to answer the question of why the world and the people in it are imperfect. I am just going to assume that we all know that it is, and you can decide on your own version of why. But, it is important to see where some of the individual expressions of imperfection or incompleteness come from. This will give you some empathy for yourself and others, as well as some clues as to why you are the way you are and what you need to do about it.

## The Early Years

OK, this is not rocket science. The CEO above was uncomfortable with confrontation, but that is not normal from the beginning of life. If you have ever talked to a two-year-old, you are aware of this. If toddlers do not like something, you are pretty much going to know about it. They have to somehow learn that to tell someone they don't like something is going to get them in trouble. When they learn that, they learn to fear confrontation and find ways to negotiate the world of relationships by avoiding it.

They learn to subtly maneuver people, manipulate them, work them, work around them, please them, or whatever it takes to make it all work. But they avoid the direct path. We will talk more about confrontation in the section on embracing and resolving the negative, but what is important now is to understand that when people lack a character ability, there is usually a good reason. In part, they learned to *not integrate that character ability into their makeup*. It could have gotten them into trouble early in life, so they avoided it and compartmentalized it instead. And, since a large part of our character is formed in our growing-up years, the early patterns are ingrained.

Or, take another example. Let's say that it is not an inability to confront that stalled out the CEO, but a fear of hurting the guy by firing him. The CEO overidentified with the one he had to put out on the streets and felt sorry for him in some way, even when he had a pattern of nonperformance and actually needed to be fired. It would have been the best thing for him, but the CEO felt too bad for him. Usually patterns like that are learned early in life, when someone grows up in a family where there is someone that the rest of the family "enables" and never holds accountable for his actions. There is an overabundance of unhelpful sympathy for the one with the problems. This is common in families where there is an addiction, for example.

But, whatever the case, in the character patterns that affect people's effectiveness, you can bet that some of them go way back in life. I once worked with one leader who always covered for nonperforming partners. He had learned that pattern in his family, as his parents made him cover for his brother who was irresponsible. Whenever he would want to pull the plug, he would feel too guilty and let it go on instead. It had become just a part of who he was, being the one who takes care of the other one who is not pulling his weight. At this point, it was affecting the way he ran his division, years past taking care of his brother.

Family, schools, churches, and friends affect people's character makeup in many different ways in the growing-up years. As we have gone through the specific areas of growth in integrity, you have probably seen some reasons why you have some gaps inside when you look at how you grew up. That is good, because it will help you get off your case and also show you what you need to do now.

One Greek word that is sometimes translated as "character" is one that means "experience." Another means "engraved mark." The experiences that you have been through have largely shaped who you are and "engraved" certain patterns and ways of behaving and responding in you. In growing up, you no doubt had some experiences that limited your development in the areas we will talk about, and some that might even have damaged those areas, like the

ones mentioned above. But, here is the good news about the corre-
lation between character and experience: *you can have new experiences
that reshape your character and engrave new patterns as well.*

As we have gone through the different dimensions of character integrity, we have talked about new experiences that will help
you grow and integrate these parts of yourself. In fact, if you remember, the section on growth involved intentionally placing
yourself in new situations that will stretch you past your current
abilities, which by definition is your past experience. And, as you
gain new experiences, those become your "past" also and thus
become part of your character. You can literally get a "new past"
by doing something new today. Tomorrow, that new experience
will be part of your past, and you will have grown. More about that
later.

## Lack of Skills Acquisition

Besides the dysfunctional experiences we have, and the compensatory patterns we develop growing up as a result of bad experience,
there is also the *lack of good experience that teaches us how to be the people we
need to be.* A bird is instinctually programmed to migrate. But, you
and I have to learn how to resolve conflict, or to exercise judgment
when our emotions are getting in the way, or to use due diligence
when we are excited about pulling the trigger on some deal. We
have to learn impulse control. We have to learn how to embrace our
own failure in a way that is motivating instead of deflating. Those
things are not instinctual in humans. In fact, they are in some ways
"counterinstinctual." We have to be trained out of the immature
patterns through discipline.

For example, where have you ever been taught the skills needed
to communicate in a way that will prevent, as much as possible,
being betrayed? Where have you been taught to relate in a way that

will have others experience you as being "for" them and will develop loyalty and trust? Or, how to observe yourself in a way that minimizes your blind spots, thus leaving you less vulnerable to failure or mistakes? These are all aspects of our character makeup that we have to be taught and disciplined to do, but often are not. If we haven't been taught, chances are we are left doing a "work-around," or overcompensating in another way, or worse, avoiding that entire area of life and work.

A close cousin to that is "modeling." Humans have a difficult time doing what we have never seen done. So, to grow in character and integrate these aspects of ourselves, we have to see it done first. We need good character models. You have probably seen, as we looked at the character model, that you sometimes did not have the real-life models that you needed in the areas where you are lacking. If you did not, then there will be deficiencies. I was working with a team of people one time and a woman brought up something another woman in the group had done that she did not like and had bothered her. The second woman responded nondefensively and wanted to understand more about how it had affected the first one. They had a really helpful conversation and solved the problem. What caught my attention, though, was a third woman in the group, who was just staring at them with a really puzzled look on her face. I asked her what was up.

"I have never seen that before," she said.

"Seen what?" I asked.

"That. She told her something that bugged her and they just worked it out."

"So? What do you mean that you haven't seen that?"

"I have never seen it work like that. Like they aren't in some big fight. They are still OK with each other. I am telling you, I have never seen that."

It took a while to unpack all of what she meant, but she was serious. Here she was, an adult career woman, and she could honestly say she had never seen how to properly have a good conflict that turned out well. Given that, how many times do you think she has directly faced into situations in her work life and gotten to resolution? She had to be shown as well as coached. But without a map in her head of how to do it, she had little chance.

## Proper Structured Feedback

We also form character as our experience is structured for us with good feedback. To grow, and to internalize new patterns, we need a "feedback loop" that sees where we are at any given level, makes us aware of it, gives us feedback with a path to do better, monitors the new changes, and repeats the cycle. That way we are internalizing not only the new skill, but the awareness and self-correction that is a necessary aspect to our performance.

This is one of the saddest things I see in leadership consulting. The "boss" relationship should be just this way: observe, give feedback, coach, monitor, and grow. Instead, too often it falls into the "ignore and zap" mentality. Bosses ignore people's patterns until the problem is too much, then they come down hard or fire them. Firing should never, ever be a surprise. It should be the end of a process (as we saw) that has attempted to give lots of corrective feedback. But when this feedback process goes right, firing does not happen, but growth does. Character thrives on feedback that is focused and used well.

## Support That Does Not Enable

In character growth, the road is sometimes rocky. We have to swallow our pride, our egos, our resistance, and sometimes just bite the bullet and hear things we don't want to hear. In that process, we can feel terrible. Almost everyone has at some time gotten feedback that was less than flattering from a superior. Sometimes it can be so tough that you either want to quit or think that you can never master what you are being told to do.

So, at those times, we also need the arm around the shoulder. We need support, and encouragement to do the hard thing. We need the push to keep going. To know that a leader or someone cares about us can help us to do the hard next step. If we know we have someone on our team, it changes everything.

But, this support has to be of a certain nature. It has to side not only with us as people, but *also with our need to grow*. The best support is also the support that cares about us but does not let us off the hook. These people do not enable us to remain the same by rescuing us, believing our excuses, explaining away our faults, or anything like that. They caringly walk alongside us, but hold us to the path at the same time.

People who have not had that can also have growth areas that have just been too difficult to tackle by themselves. They might have seen or been told about those parts of themselves, but it seemed too difficult, discouraging, or frightening to face alone. Or they might have had support at the times they have seen them, but their supporters just blamed other people for the mistakes or did other things to let them off the hook. So, the support actually enabled them to avoid the growth that was needed, instead of empowering them to go through it. That is the kind we need for character growth. Without it, avoidance too often takes over.

## Practice Without Catastrophic Results

I remember a leader once telling me the day that he decided that he would never trust anyone again. He had once been put in a new situation and had wanted to learn to be part of a real team. He had opened himself up to some people in the new situation and had been betrayed in an awful way. This had been years before, and he had never regained that ability. As a result, his leadership tended to go down the path of the lone ranger, and it was affecting his ability to reach his goals. He was cut off from the power of leverage that relationships and alliances give. But, without the ability to trust, it was not going to happen.

If he was ever going to get past his level of performance, he was going to have to get over playing it so close to the vest. But, when he thought of doing this, he got really uncomfortable. He had to control all information, was afraid to delegate, fearful of not seeing everything, and a little suspicious anytime he was "out of the loop." This is not the way that high performers operate, and he was going to have to learn to trust, as well as confide in others. But the chances are slim that he is going to do that in a high-risk situation again. He needed a safe place to regain trust.

If you have not had a safe place to develop different aspects of who you are, and to practice in ways that your career or life is not at risk, you have probably not developed certain character traits. *In some ways, you have been in survival mode, and that is not the mode in which we usually develop new aspects of character, other than perseverance.* Too much protection is going on when you are just trying to survive. New skills require openness, but survival requires protecting oneself, and to some degree, not being open. That is why in fear-based corporate cultures, people often do not grow in new ways. They are too busy guarding themselves and watching their back.

We have seen some new skills throughout this book that you can practice. But for now, just know that if you have only been in survival and protection mode, it will help explain why there may be some gaps. In the same way that technical skills are built through training and practice, so are character abilities.

## Improper Motivation

Sometimes aspects of personal and character development are seen as something we "ought to do." We think things like, "Yeah, I need to be a better Boy Scout and go to a personal-development retreat, or coach, when I get the time." To some degree, most people have moments when they think that they should be doing some sort of life review, or inventory, and thinking about ways that they could be better. In those moments, they might even "want to want to" make some plans. But, usually, the things that we only think we "ought" to do, or "it would be good to do," give way to the needs of the urgent things that our lives and performance demands are asking us to do. We are too busy "doing" what we need to do to ever become whom we need to be. As a result, because we don't become whom we need to be, in the end we don't do the things we need to do. We live upside-down lives.

The long and the short of it is that "ought to" has never been a good motivator for humans, at least in the areas of character that are underdeveloped. In the more mature parts of ourselves, we usually do what we ought to do. But it is because those things have *become a part* of us, and we express them freely. We are truly "doing" what we have become in our character. However, to the extent that some trait is not yet truly who we are, the "ought to" do those things usually lasts about as long as a New Year's resolution or as long as someone is nagging us or on our case. Ultimately, we will also resist that.

So, what does motivate us to develop character where we do not have it? *Reality losses, rewards, and consequences.* You see character change when people have to finally face the reality that their lack of ability in some area is costing them. The alcoholic does not get treatment until the spouse and kids throw him or her out. The nonexerciser doesn't get healthy until the heart attack. Both have been told that they "ought to do better." But change does not hit until reality does.

People change when they "play the movie," which is to take a hard reality look at your life and work, then play that reality forward to see if you like the way the future movie of your life and career plays out. In that way, people begin to experience the future losses, rewards, and consequences right now and get with reality. When you look, for example, at your present performance, and the things that you are not getting, and then you realize that if you continue to do the same things expecting different results, you will *never get what you want,* you will change. When you truly get it, that your lack of growth in some area is what is keeping you from having what you desire in life, then you will develop that ability. It may be in your career or in your personal life, either one.

You see this in relationships when people finally realize that they have some pattern that they need to change. They go through a divorce or pick the fifth boyfriend in a row who cannot commit. Then, they wake up: "There is something about me that I have to change if I am ever going to find lasting love." And they go work on it. They find that they are too passive or adaptive or defensive or controlling, and that is why they are not finding the love that they need. They finally stop blaming it on the outside world and get to work on themselves. No matter what the outside world is like, they finally realize that is reality, and they develop the character to meet the demands of that reality in the relational setting. It is the playing the movie forward and seeing one more failed relationship in their future if they do not develop in some way.

If you are going to grow and develop or help someone else, you will have to get out of the "ought to's" and into reality. When you realize that you are only going to get what you desire in love or work through the character growth that is needed, you will get to work. Not before. So, if you have never been in a place where it was safe to face reality, or where you had the need to face it, or had the help to face it, that may be part of why there are gaps.

## The Heart

You have heard it said a thousand different ways:

Anyone can change, but they have to want to.

You can lead a horse to water, but you can't make him drink.

How many psychologists does it take to change a lightbulb? One, but the lightbulb has to really want to change.

He just doesn't want to look at the truth. He is in denial.

She wants to blame everyone else, but not take a look at herself.

Throughout time, there have always been ways that observers of human nature have expressed a certain truth: you cannot make a person change who does not want to. Now, that said, we also saw above that *we can do a LOT to make someone "want to."* Consequences can motivate someone previously not motivated. Love and support can do the same. New opportunity or a new environment of growth and ingredients previously not available can do that as well. We *can* influence previously unmotivated people to change. You can actually get them to "want to," to some degree, *if they want to.*

If that sounds like a paradox or an oxymoron or a contradiction or whatever, it is. It is a fundamental truth of human existence that we are both determined and autonomous. We have things that can influence us, and we also have fundamental existential freedom and responsibility whereby we are ultimately responsible for ourselves, no excuses where we can say "the devil made me do it."

So, call it timing, or heart, but some people are just not either ready to change or don't want to. They just take a stance in life whereby they do not want to be different and just want the world to adapt to them instead of vice versa. As the founders of AA said, for those people they were not able to offer much help.

In our list of where the gap in character comes from, we just have to include this reality: some people have integrity and growth issues because they are unwilling to make the shifts that character demands. They kind of "flip off" reality, the light, wisdom, or whatever influence comes into their lives. They have a stance that is past resistance and is defiant. For them, we can try to motivate, but ultimately, they have to make a choice. If you are reading this book, hopefully that is not you, and you want to see where you need to grow. But, it is a reality for some, and if you are trying to help someone, and he is not responding after many attempts by you to help, he may just be resistant. You might do better to spend your time with someone who really wants to change.

## Genes, Experiences, and Choices

OK, I did not mention your genes. I guess that at some level we have to say "pick your parents well." There is some truth in that someone's constitutional makeup and temperament have bearing on their character issues. If you go into a nursery at any hospital, you can almost see the ones who are going to be initiators, and the ones who are going to "go with the flow." The sad truth is that to some degree, some of their necessary growth paths are already awaiting them. The passive ones are going to have to work harder on being direct and assertive, and the screamers are going to one day have to learn to go against their nature and shut up and listen. Genes are real determinants of behavior.

There is not a lot you can do about what you started with, to somehow change your history. Your genetic makeup is what it is. But here is the reality: your life has *many* determinants, and you are responsible for dealing with them. Your genes/temperament are two of those determinants. So is your past experience, and so are the choices that you have made along the line. Your character integrity is a combination of all of those things together, i.e., the cards you have been dealt and how you have played them. You can work with your constitutional weaknesses just as you can work with other determinants.

If you find it tough to initiate, for example, then there are probably many determinants for that. Maybe you are by temperament more of a follower, or maybe you had a domineering parent or sibling or relative who was mean to you every time you took an initiating step. As a result, you chose to go with the flow and have continued that passive path in life and work. There are a million reasons why we are the way we are.

The question now, in adult life, is *What are we going to do about it?* Your makeup now is what it is, and it is either serving you well in some areas or not. If you like the wake and are able to meet the demands that reality is asking you to meet in some areas, that is great, and life has been good to you in those areas or you have worked it out. But, in the places where it is not going as well, no matter what caused it, you are the one who is able to get with the program now and make a change.

You can alter your experience and you can make new choices that build the kind of character that is going to enable you to meet the demands of reality. You can learn the kinds of experiences that you need to build new abilities, and the kinds of choices that you can make. The promise is that as you grow, you can negotiate more and more of the realities that you face and, as you do, realize more of who you were created to be.

So, as we end our journey looking at integrity, there are a few takeaway points that I would like you to keep in mind:

- Integrity is not something that you either "have or don't have." You probably have aspects where you do, and parts where you don't.

- You might think that the high achievers somehow have it all together, but they don't.
- All of us have issues in our character that are great opportunities for growth and development. You are not bad, inadequate, or somehow defective because of that. You are human. Accept it, embrace it, and let's get on the journey.
- When you understand where character comes from, you can better understand and accept why you and some others that you know have some gaps inside. It makes perfect sense why you are missing some abilities.
- Also, when you understand where character comes from, you begin to get a glimpse of the kinds of things that are going to help you grow.
- And lastly, there is hope. When you get motivated by the reality desires that you have and realize that changes can bring those to fruition, you can get moving and see results.

If you look at all of the causes mentioned in this chapter, there is great news. Other than your genes, you can change all of the causes of the "chinks" in your armor. You can grow in integrity. In fact, I think that all of life is a journey to develop more integrated character, for everyone. Each situation that we find ourselves in, each "reality demand," calls us to take that step to become more than who we already are, as we have seen.

Look at the list again:

- The early years of life
- Lack of skills acquisitions
- Lack of structured feedback
- Lack of support that does not enable
- Lack of practice in a safe setting

- Lack of proper motivation
- Lack of a heart's desire to change
- Genes, experiences, and choices

As a consultant and a psychologist, I can tell you that people overcome and change every one of these on a regular basis. None of them is fixed forever. Even "the early years," your past experience, can be healed and changed by getting new experiences that give you the love, support, validation, and healing that you did not get the first time around. In a good growth group, or community, you can literally find the growth "family" that gives you what you might have missed.

The rest of the list is like that as well. Through the kinds of structured growth experiences that we saw (in chapter 11, Getting Better All the Time), you can find the answers to all of them. Workshops, training, therapy, groups, mentors, spiritual disciplines, and all of those things we talked about, can integrate your character to heights you never thought possible. It is done every day. All it takes is opening up to those kinds of growth experiences and investing yourself. In the same ways that your material investments grow as they are put to use, so does your character. Invest in growth in yourself, and let time compound the interest.

Also, I want to add one other note when thinking about how to grow in integrity of character: keep the six traits that I listed on p. xii in mind as you invest yourself. Invest in them specifically, because they are all integrated. They work together and will pay dividends to each other as you use all of them.

For example, the more you develop trust with people, the more secure you will be, and able to take the blinders off and see reality. And vice versa, the more you see reality, the more you will be able to trust good people. You will not be so afraid and suspicious. You will see the good ones for who they are.

Then, the more you see reality, the more you will be able to access what really works and get better results. Your fruitfulness will improve because you will be operating in the world as it really is, and that is where profits are made. The people who see the truth are the ones who always score. And, as you do that, you will become more effective and charge into dealing with negatives like never before. Vice versa, as you engage those problems, you get better results, see more reality, and people trust you more. The circle of integration gets larger, and your heart, mind, and soul expand.

Whenever that happens, people begin to invest in the bigger picture, and develop more of a transcendent character. As they do that, they are more trustworthy, see more reality, get better results, engage problems better and so forth. In short, integration begets more integration. So, as you invest yourself in all aspects of the model, you will benefit exponentially.

As I work with leaders and those who accomplish great things, the things that they achieve are certainly fun and fulfilling. "A desire accomplished is sweet to the soul," as the Jewish proverb says. But the further along the path they go, I also see that the personal growth and development that occurs within them and in their relationships is what becomes more and more invigorating over time. As their character grows, and they increasingly give themselves to transcendent realities, the journey gets richer and more fulfilling. Integrity brings many rewards, many riches, and many fruits. But, in the end, it is a reward in and of itself. That is my prayer for you, that as you grow, you may enjoy integrity's fruits in a multifold manner, and that you will enjoy it for itself as well.

# index

"ought to," 275–77
overidentification, 59
ownership, and embracing the negative,
     185–88, 195

pain, and embracing the negative,
     198–200
paranoia, 81
parent-toddler group (example), 153–54
parents, alcohol or abusive, 178–79
partnership, Sheila-Sarah (example),
     68–71
passion
   and growth, 216, 217
   and making connections, 53, 54, 62
Peck, Scott, 172
performance ceilings, 11
perseverance
   and getting results, 156–59, 160
   and growth, 205
   and transcendence, 240
playing fair, 82–84
power, 87–96
practice
   and "chinks in the armor," 273–74, 280
   in safe setting, 280
   without catastrophic results, 273–74
problems
   avoiding, 173–79
   and character as interaction of factors,
      282
   and characteristics of character, 9
   confronting/facing, 173–79, 191–94,
      195, 200
   and embracing the negative, 171–200
   expense of, 15–16
   and growth, 206–8
   and integrity, 35, 36, 38
   and letting go of bad stuff, 194–95
   and ownership, 185–88
   and reality, 13–16
   and recoverability, 180–83
   separating from, 183–85, 187
   solving, 35, 36, 195–98, 206–8
Proctor and Gamble China venture
   (example), 112–13

projecting, 122–23
psychiatric-hospital industry (example),
     156–59, 171–72, 247–48
psychosis, 241
The Purpose Driven Life (Warren), 111–12,
     149–50

readiness, 196
ready, aim, fire, 147–53
reality
   and accommodation, 133–38
   and assimilation, 133–38
   avoiding, 107–8, 114–15, 120–23
   blocks to seeing, 126
   and building trust, 79, 86
   and character as interaction of factors,
      281–82
   and "chinks in the armor," 275–77, 278,
      279
   and definition and characteristics of
      character, 9, 22
   and embracing the negative, 172, 173
   emotional investment in, 114–15
   and extending favor, 79, 86
   and feedback from others, 116–20
   as friend, 106, 112
   gap between ideal and, 37–39
   getting in touch with, 99–110
   and getting results, 152
   and integrity, 35, 37–41
   and invalidation, 63–64
   and making connections, 63–64, 70,
      71–73
   and motivation, 275–77
   and observing ego, 123–25
   and problems, 13–16
   relationship of character and, 23–28
   seeking, 112–23
   and splitting, 131–33
   and transcendence, 240, 245, 255–56
   and truth, 113, 115, 125–27
   and unmerited help, 86
   and vulnerability, 88, 95
   of wake, 16–21
   See also meeting demands of reality
Reality Therapy, 232–33

# BOOKS BY DR. HENRY CLOUD

## INTEGRITY
### The Courage to Meet the Demands of Reality

ISBN 978-0-06-084969-6 (paperback)

In this groundbreaking book, Dr. Cloud shows what integrity is, how it is lived in everyday experience, and how to determine whether you are perceived as someone with character and integrity.

## THE ONE-LIFE SOLUTION
### Reclaim Your Personal Life While Achieving Greater Professional Success

ISBN 978-0-06-146643-4 (paperback)

Dr. Cloud extends his bestselling formula to the workplace and convincingly demonstrates that setting physical, mental, emotional, and spiritual boundaries at work is not only helpful, but essential to establishing a successful, happy, and rewarding career.